THE REMINISCENCES OF THE OLD INTELLIGENT

With Folklore and Poems

Vladimir G. Loos

authorHOUSE®

AuthorHouse™
1663 Liberty Drive
Bloomington, IN 47403
www.authorhouse.com
Phone: 1-800-839-8640

First published by AuthorHouse 1/25/2010

ISBN: 978-1-4490-6902-5 (e)
ISBN: 978-1-4490-6901-8 (sc)

Library of Congress Control Number: 2009914358

Printed in the United States of America
Bloomington, Indiana

This book is printed on acid-free paper.

CONTENTS

To my dear wife Natasha

INTRODUCTION

"What was nice and pleased my soul
Slipped away long time ago..."
(From the very popular Russian song of 30th)

This book is about ridiculous and very serious things of Soviet realities. It is intended for American reader.

At the end of the narration the reader will find the *Vocabulary* of specific names and terms as well as the geographic names.

After the *Vocabulary* a reader will find the *Name Directory* which includes in alphabetical order all mentioned in the text names (look for the last names which are wrote in bold). Russian names have a format: last name, first name and patronymic name.

Cited books are placed in the *Literature* at the very end of the book (the names of the books are written in italic).

Every anecdote is marked out by the braces.

The author of this book had immigrated to the USA from the former Soviet Union in 1995. He was born and lived in the Kiev City, the capital of the Ukraine Soviet Socialistic Republic (in the structure of the former Soviet Union), now the independent State of Ukraine.

Author worked in the USA more than twelve years, associated with many Americans, and developed the impression that Americans do not truly understand the mentality and the soul of the "Russian Bear".

However, much more crucial that Americans mostly misunderstand the soviet realities, the times of the Communists ruling in the Soviet Union (1917-1990) in spite of the novels of **Solzhenitsyn**, the **Pasternak**'s *Doctor Zhivago* and many other disclosures.

The Communist Party of the Soviet Union (CPSU) has not been a subject of a criminal trial, and now nothing has cardinally changed in the Russia: the same humiliation of personality, the lack of protection of private property.

The acquaintance of the Americans with soviet times' folklore, realities, some Russian and Ukrainian poetry would serve for better understanding of the danger of any socialist and communist ideas, for better understanding the enigmatic "Russian Soul" which is deep, complicated, easily wounded, and very-very broad.

Not so long ago Americans got an opportunity to be acquainted with the book of Ben **Lewis** about the humor in the communist countries, which is very interesting, has a lot of witty jokes.

My book is completely different by its content and orientation. Me, an old intelligent, was born in the Soviet Union and had an opportunity to watch its realities by own eyes from the day of the birth. The book includes many anecdotes on different topics, not only so named "anti-Soviet anecdotes".

WHO IS AN INTELLIGENT

For Russia this word means a lot. According to the high standards of Russian mentality, an intelligent is the person who is educated enough, polite, can be told by his empathy to other people, animals, by his positive habits to dress, to communicate, by his behavior in society; and for male intelligent - by his attitude toward women.

<Ivan Ivanovich[1], tell me about the difference between an old and a contemporary intelligent.

O.K.: The old intelligent was always a little bit drunk, clean shaven and knew from **Bach** to **Feuerbach**.

The contemporary intelligent is always a little bit shaven, drunk as a lord, and knows from barbecue to damn you.>

"Every family has its own black sheep," as the popular Russian proverb says.

<**Pushkin** , "the sun of the Russian poetry", perished in a duel protecting the honor of a woman.

Mayakovskiy, "the singer of the Socialist Revolution", has shot himself because of a woman.

Docent (the assumed last name) – the Assistant Professor of the University) used foul language addressing to a woman.>

---

1   Ivan Ivanovich - the most popular Russian first and patronymic names.

The person who wants to become an intelligent not necessary has to descend from a good stock, to graduate Harvard or Moscow University. The next anecdote was told me by my father who was born in an ordinary family. He taught me to be polite, to learn, to kiss a woman's hand, to make way and place for a woman and older adult, so to be the real intelligent.

<Question: What an erudite person must be able? Answer: He must be able to distinguish **Gogol** from **Hegel**, **Hegel** from **Bebel**, **Bebel** from **Babel**, **Babel** from a cable, cable from 'kobel', 'kobel' from a bitch.>

(kobel – a male-dog in the Russian language).

I think many parents would prefer their child to become an intelligent. At the same time I suppose that this is a hard task to raise an intelligent. Think and choose. The next anecdote is about the "purified" intelligent again.

<Streetcar is overcrowded. Old woman is standing, while all seats are occupied by the young men reading newspapers.

Old woman is just saying: "The times have badly changed. There is no intelligent anymore."

After some silence one man tears himself away a newspaper, takes off glasses and replies:

"You make a mistake, grand-mother. There are as many intelligent as a trash. But there is a big shortage of the seats.">

"He is a good father, just as he is a good son. Personally, he walks straightly, resembling in this his forerunner **Nietzsche**. He is a man with a well-balanced and strongly personality. He is austere towards others and anything but indulgent where his own case is concerned; and, for all his severity, he displays that old-fashioned Austrian courtesy which is now threatened with extinction."

This is about great **Freud** from the book of his disciple Fritz **Wittels**.

And let us go back to Russia. One real Russian intelligent about the other real Russian intelligent: "I certify with all my heart that he was a person with an uncommon inner generosity, breeding and refinement in the best meaning of these words, with gentleness and tact, having at the same time an unusual sincerity and simplicity, sensitiveness and tenderness with a rare veracity." It was the words of great Ivan Alekseyevich **Bunin** about great Anton Pavlovich **Chekhov**.

So, the main reason of this book is not just to smile or to laugh.

RUSSIAN MENTALITY

Russia has many outstanding poets: **Pushkin,
Lermontov, Nekrasov, Esenin**. They were great because
could feel the Russian soul. One more Russian poet,
Tyutchev, is not so great in the people's memory but well
known for every Russian intelligent. He wrote in 1866:

> "You cannot seize the Russian soul.
> Just using your mind.
> You cannot seize the Russian soul
> Just using common measure.
> The Russia has her own pride
> She only can be trusted.

<Two tape-worms, Father and Son, crept out of an anus.
"Dad, look," rapturously exclaimed Son. "What a beauty!
The sun is shining, the birds are chirping, the sky is blue."
"You are right, Sonny. But our Motherland is inside,"
father answered.>

This is true. Many Russians lived and live now being
very poor and humiliated. But they are real patriots of their
Motherland which treats them so badly. **Napoleon** and
Hitler had an opportunity to learn this for a sure.

Before 1990 the communists seized all benefits, being
secretly rich and very arrogant. After 1990 many of them
remaining arrogant changed their social orientation, began to

be newborn nabobs and religiously obedient. It was the turn on 180 degrees. Big money and trust in God valued in the civilized world were strictly prohibited for the communists.

Andropov began his activity as a General Secretary of the Communist Party of the Soviet Union in 1982 trying to increase a labor discipline. He issued a secret order: to stop on the streets during the day time the people who have to be at the working places and to convey them to the police. Police informed a human resources department of the facility where the person worked. Then the punishment would go: to decrease a salary, to denounce in a labor discipline violation.

That time anecdote.

<A woman-employee comes to her supervisor and asks his permission to leave during the working time because her mother is arriving from the other city, and she wants to see her.

Supervisor does not believe and keeps refusing. At last the woman resorts to the extreme measure and gets the whole thing off her chest: she wants to meet her lover.

"This is quite a different thing!" supervisor is becoming to be animated. "But no shopping, go straight to the bed.">

Many Russians have a strong sense of humor. Here is the next anecdote.

<A military squad is disassembling an old building. A sergeant-major is walking in front of standing soldiers.

"Private **Ivanov**[2], what are you thinking about?" the sergeant-major asks.

---

2   Ivanov, Petrov, Sidorov – Russian wide-spread last names.

"I am thinking that on this place will be built a Palace of Labor, and the soviet people would enjoy this new modern building," **Ivanov** answers.

"Good. And you, private **Petrov**?"

"I am thinking about the new comfortable flats instead of the old ones where soviet people will enjoy their life," **Petrov** answers.

"Excellent," the sergeant-major keeps walking and talking.

"And you, private **Sidorov**. What are you thinking about?"

"I am thinking about a woman, comrade sergeant-major."

The sergeant-major is perplexed.

"What? Why?"

"Because I am always thinking about a woman, comrade sergeant-major," private **Sidorov** is answering.>

Military anecdotes are very popular in Russia. Usually they depict the officers not to the best advantage.

<A military squad is doing the construction works. A sergeant-major makes command: "You need to dig a trench from here till the lunch.">

<The ball is in full swing in the 19th century Russia. Two generals are standing by the wall, not dancing. Ball manager comes to them:

"Gentlemen, why you are not dancing, I ask you to dance."

One general answers: "Pardon, sir. We are not the dancers. We are the sex-machines.">

The Russians are very proud. Overtly they have to obey officials, but the ones must have a lot of positives to be respected. Let us go to the next anecdote.

<Outside is the bright summer morning.
General Secretary of the Communist Party of the Soviet Union Leonid Ilyich **Brezhnev** is coming out on the balcony. He is met by the caressing sun.

"Good morning, serene Sun,"- **Brezhnev** greets the sun.

"Good morning, Leonid Ilyich," the sun is answering.

In the evening **Brezhnev** is coming out on the balcony and seeing the sun that is going to the horizon.

"Good night, tired sun," he says.

"Go to the hell, rascal. I am in the West now," the sun is answering.>

Brezhnev was a controversial enough figure. He was very handsome in his good years, and many women dreamed to have a child from him. Now in the Russia the movies about him and his daughter Galina were shot. Anyhow to reach the highest position in the great country someone has to have the special abilities. However, many anecdotes (contrary to the movies) do not treat **Brezhnev** with a duly respect. Like this one.

<In 2030 a teacher asks high school students: "Who was Leonid Ilyich **Brezhnev**?"

The answer of an excellent pupil: "Small states-man from the epoch of Alla **Pugacheva**.">
(Very famous Russian pop-singer)

The previous General Secretary of the Communist Party of the Soviet Union **Khrushchev** is well-known in the West, especially in the United States. Here the anecdote about him.

<Khrushchev came to the Moscow modern art exhibition. He is looking at the abstract paintings, getting more and more furies, passing from one picture to another using the obscene words. At last he is stopping and beginning to stare at the wall.

"And what the buttock is this?" he asks.

"This is a mirror, comrade **Khrushchev,**" a manager of the exhibition answers (abstract art was tabooed by soviet ideology as well as all things which were incomprehensible for Communist party bigwigs).>

Khrushchev made a lot of bad and good things. The most prominent deed he accomplished - releasing of many political prisoners from the Soviet concentration camps. But the artists could not forgive his brutal, arrogant and humiliating criticism of the modern art.

The protection of one's own dignity is the one of the strongest trait of the Russian people.

<Meeting of the Communist party's local organization is in action. The members are discussing an amoral deed of their colleague, comrade **Ivanov**, whose wife found a woman's underpants in the pocket of his trousers.

After a general condemnation the local party leader asks **Ivanov**:

"Did you completely understand?"

"Sure, I did," **Ivanov** answers.

"What did you understand?"

"Next time I am going to take the underpants off from one woman's leg.">

Many Russians usually do not pay attention to the trifles of life, use to think by the broad categories. Here are the next two anecdotes.

<Rocket company commander has returned after vacations. During his absence an extraordinary incident has happened.

Several soldiers drank a lot of vodka and began to make drunken amusements during which they pushed a special button, and have started a rocket on one foreign country.

The commander formed up the company and began to walk angrily to and fro. Then he said:

"I do not care about the country but I want to know when the order would be in the company.">

<International car races came to the end. The procedure of reward is beginning.

Announcer: "The third prize was won by the racer from the Great Britain, mister **Donaldson.** It is a luxury car."

Music, ovation is coming.

"Second prize was won by the Russian racer, mister **Ivanov.** He won a right to kiss a hand of the beautiful lady."

Lady is coming forward.

Ivanov indignantly: "What are you talking about? What the lady. I want more than a kiss!" Announcer interferes: "Excuse me, Sir, but this is the first prize.">

Now I would like to talk about the ability to find the best decision in any circumstances.

<A schoolboy missed a week in an elementary school. A woman-teacher asks him to explain his absenteeism. The school-boy makes the explanations.

On Monday my mother has washed my underpants. On Tuesday on my way to school I saw your underpants that dried outside on the rope.

On Wednesday going to school I saw a coin on the ground, stepped on it and waited when the passers-by stop walking to pick the coin up.

On Thursday my father was bringing our cow to the bull.

Teacher: 'Couldn't your father do it by himself?'

Schoolboy: 'Surely, he could. But a bull can do it better.

On Friday I made a demand: 'I am not going to school until Chile Junta releases **Corvalan**.' ">

Russian ordinary people have a very broad and kind soul.

Great Russian poet **Nekrasov** wrote:

> If pity, do it carefully,
> Don't probe a peasant-laborer
> With landlord's subtle measurement!
> We are not tender lazy bones,
> We are great people everywhere
> When work or revelry.

(The poem *Who is Happy in Russia?*, written in 1873-1876)

Here is the real life episode during celebration of New Year's Eve. There three o'clock in the morning, in the room is the big table full of viands. Strong Russian male about 35 years old who has already drunk a lot of vodka becomes more and more agitated. He proposes everybody to lay a wager that he would drink the full bottle of vodka (0.5 liter) at a stretch drinking straight from the bottle. So, he takes stand on the table, uncorks the bottle, inserts a neck of the bottle directly to his throat and poured out the full bottle of vodka at a stretch. He was not knocked from his feet but began to be very aggressive.

This is not a secret for anybody that Russians drink a lot. Why? Why so much? It's another question for another time.

In many occasions the drinking is an expression of the joy of life – "the festivity of the soul". The festivity however occurs often enough on the highest notes: aggressive behavior, strong obscene language, unpredictable actions. Now there are two more anecdotes.

<The well gone jolly crowd of the Russian people is on the spree in the restaurant. A waiter comes up and asks: "Gentlemen, how do you like me to serve a baby-pig: with a horseradish or without?"

One man from the crowd: "Listen, pal, cut off the horseradish and bring us just a baby-pig."

(Baby-pig is usually served with a horseradish; here is a pun: in Russian language one word is used for a horseradish and for a penis)>

< One of the Russian celebrities is in the last stage of intoxication.

Drunk as a lord he is coming upon the door of his apartment and ringing the bell. His wife is opening. He says: "Pal, let's drink a little bit more vodka and go to the women!>

The Russian male is very kind, intentionally polite and witty when being in the intermediate stage of the alcohol intoxication. One of the very first toasts that proposed at the drinking table: "Let's meet under the table!" Here is the next anecdote.

<The prostitute house in Paris is in fire. Shouts: 'Fire! Bring the water!'
Voice of the Russian customer: 'And two mugs of beer!'>

"In the Russia there is a gaiety of drinking," - one ancient sage told once upon a time. There are two more anecdotes.

<Russian man will never say "I drank yesterday for nothing!" He can either say "I did not need to mix a vodka with a beer!", or "I did not need to drink without getting a bite!", or "I did not need to drink with those persons!", or "I did not need to drink out of home!" But he will never say "For nothing!">

<One hundred grams[3] of Russian vodka can substitute one hour of meditation, and after drinking the half liter of vodka all chakras are having been open and the third eye begins to see beauty in every woman.>

Russian mentality is not only overtly oriented but also has the deep ends. Here are some sayings.

---

3   One hundred grams – the most modest Russian dose of vodka when drinking (1/10 of liter; 1 quart U.S. = 0.946 liter). A half liter of vodka – often the beginning of drinking in Russia.

<Why do you hate me so much? I had never ever done anything good for you.>

<Protect me from the friends. I shall get rid of the enemies by myself.>

The last saying I heard from the Assistant Professor of Kiev City State University who was forced to leave.

At the end of this part of the book - the famous Russian maxims:

<If it's impossible, but somebody wants it so much, then it's possible.>

<There is nothing of good when a crowbar is used…
if there is no other crowbar.>

<I cannot put your 'Thank you' in a pocket, pour it in a glass.>

<The sea, give a way - the trash is floating.>

<20 years old: if there is no mind, so there would not be any.
30 years old: if there is no wife, so there would not be the one.
40 years old: if there is no money, so there would not be any.>

<All diseases come from the nerves, only syphilis is derived from the pleasure.>

<If you have strength you do not need a mind.>

And then some pearls from the drinking area.

<Knocked back in the morning - all day long is free.>

<If vodka interferes with a work, throw your work up.>

<Water is not like vodka, you cannot drink it too much.>

<If you drink vodka without beer – you throw money at random.>

WOMEN

We talked till now about serious things. Let's choose something pleasant.

Russian women are excellent in many respects. Nobody can say better about Russian woman than Russian poet. So, the great **Nekrasov** again:

> In Russia villages women
> Bear calmly importance in face,
> Have beautiful strength in their motions,
> With gate and a glance of Empress,-

They only by blind wouldn't be noticed,
And seeing is eager to say:
"When passed - as if sun she turned lighter!
If glanced – like by rouble[4] endowed!"
(from the poem *The Red-Nosed Frost*, written in 1863).

Many Russian women have no cars and are forced to use public transportation.

<Three women share their feelings how they are getting to the working place.
First woman: "I go by a trolleybus. You cannot believe that every day my buttons are torn off."

---

4   Rouble – Russian currency.

Second woman: "Your problem worth nothing. I go by a bus. And every day I am ashamed to come to the office: my clothes are badly trampled."

Third woman: "I would like to have your problems, ladies. I go by train, and every two months I am forced to do an abortion.">

Russian women's mentality is very touching; but maybe all women in the world have no difference in the peculiarity of their logic.

<If a woman says "No" - it means "May be."
If a woman says "May be" - it means "Yes."
If a woman says "Yes"– she is not a real woman.>

Woman's logic is so specific. The psychologist could describe this logic as directed to the self-defense.

<Husband says to his wife during their controversy: "Why are you yelling?"
Wife: "What did you say? You said that I am barking. Oh, so, I am a dog."
Shouting to her mother: "Mother, he named me a bitch!">

One more example of woman's logic by a word of the former first lady, the wife of **Khrushchev** - Nina Petrovna **Khrushcheva**, very decent, by the way, mother and spouse.

<Nina Petrovna is coming home after shopping.
"You know, husband,"- she says with surprise. - "Just yesterday you were dismissed from the post of the General Secretary of the CPSU and today all stores are empty.">

Here is one more anecdote about the logic of a common Russian woman.

<The husband returns home and sees that a lodger is sleeping with his wife.

He tears the lodger off the wife and punches him strongly in the face. The lodger becomes unconscious and falls on the floor.

"You are right, man," says the wife to the husband. "He does not pay rent and moreover – sleeps with me."

After a while the lodger comes to himself and punches the husband who becomes unconscious.

"You are right, pal," wife says to the lodger. "He does not sleep with me by himself and prohibits others to do this.">

Russian woman is lovely, especially inwardly. She has so much dignity for herself and devotion for the person whom she really loves.

Here is the verse of famous Russian poet Demyan **Bedny**.

TAN'KA[5]

Through the country noisy rumor wander,
Peasant women cannot be tired of talking:
As if Tan'ka met over the forest
Komsomolez[6] **Korotkov**, Grigoriy.
What is up? Whom touches this matter
What young couple doing over forest.
Just the women's envy is tremendous –
No more love, and nothing left to boast.

---

5   Tan'ka – rough Russian first name for Tatyana, Tanya.

6   Komsomolez – name for the member of the Youth Communist Union of the USSR.

Their whole life be stove tied,
Owned by husbands coarse and cruel,
So they gad through huts about
And keep smearing lovely girl.
Through the country noisy rumor wandered,
Swimming with no boat and no oars.
As if Tan'ka having been abandoned,
And turned grey with badly grief and sorrow.

Here is the situation from the real life. Afternoon, 5p.m. A large crowd of women is gathering outside an exit checkpoint of one of the Moscow big motor-car works. Many women came with small children. To-day is a pay-day. The women are waiting for their husbands. It is necessary to meet a spouse and to take away the greatest part of his salary needy for family living; otherwise the money will be squander on drink the same day.

Russian woman is of a great endurance.
Outstanding Russian poet **Nekrasov**:
Exceptional beauty – let world be amazed,
Is ruddy, and slender, and tall,
Good looking - any garments she wears,
Dexterous - any work she performs.
She stands either hunger or cold,
She's always so patient and calm.
I saw how she moves her scythe down:
One sweep and a haycock is done!
In play even horse-man can't catch her,
When trouble - no fear - she'll save:
She'll rein up full galloping horse,
And step into house on fire! (From poem *The Red-Nosed Frost*, 1863)

Russian women have contributed their country seriously for a victory in the World War II both at the battle-front and at the home front.

<World War II, winter, bitter cold.

A general travels through front army line positions and saw a soldier.

"Are you frozen" - the general asks.

"Yes, comrade general, I did" - the soldier answers.

"And your cock is frozen too?"

"Definitely, not, comrade general" the soldier is answering. "I am a woman".>

Certainly, in Russia, in Ukraine, as in any other country, exists jealousy, unfaithfulness, most often when married couple are temporarily parted due vacation, business trip. Very good opportunity for an affair is in Russian Miami - Sochi, in Yalta at the Crimea, in other resorts.

<Foreigner: "I am interested, are there the prostitution houses in the Soviet Union?"

Expert: "Yes, but they are taken away from the borders of the city and called for some reason the 'rest houses'">

<A husband is seeing of his wife who is going to the resort.

He stands beside the train. The wife is inside the train behind a closed window.

They are looking at each other. The train is about to move.

Out of the blue the husband realizes that he did not say the main thing.

"Do not sleep with anybody,"- he is shouting.

"I do not understand,"- the wife is answering through the closed window.

"Do not sleep with anybody,"- the husband shouts again much louder.

"I still do not understand,"- the wife shouts back.

The train begins to move.

The husband is walking and trying to shout much louder.

All of a sudden he runs by his head against the electrical post.

"Do what you want ," he is yelling.

"Understood ," the wife is yelling in respond.>

<Sometimes Russian woman happens to drink an alcohol. The experts discern three stages of her intoxication.

The first: "O! What a tipsy I am!!!"

The second: "Who is drunk!? I am - drunk!?"

The third: When answering to a taxi driver 'Where to go?' she bangs him on the head by her handbag and says: "This is not of your business, brute!">

At the end of the topic a couple of sobriquets due to women's extravagant hair- do.

<I have fallen from a dump truck, put the brakes by my head.>

<I am my Mommy's little foolish girl.>

MEN AND WOMEN

Where is a woman, there is a man. Here is the anecdote about men's logic.

<A group of men is standing on the street.
Lovely young woman is going by.
One man to another: "Did you sleep with her?"
Other man: "No. And you?"
First man: "Neither do I."
Together: "What a bitch!">

Naturally there are many jokes regarding sexual intercourse – scabrous (salty) jokes. The strongest one, I suppose.

<A marmoset for bear made a sweet minet[7].
Morals:
No morals.
No more marmoset.
And bear's member lost a half of male set.">

In our youth we supposed shameful just to talk about a minet. Our friendly circle considered this kind of sex as humiliating, first of all for a woman. But times have changed, mostly owing to the evolution of the society on the

---

7   Minet (French) – oral sex when woman plays an active role (see the books of
     Ian **Kerner** in the *Literature*).

base of psychoanalytic achievements, especially the works of Sigmund **Freud**.

Mankind knows now for a sure that there are several erotogenic zones, including mouth area. May be mankind also knows that a masturbation makes nothing bad.

From the book of Fritz **Wittels** again: "Masturbation is neither a vice nor a disease, but a normal form of human sexual activity. Per se, it is harmless. Had Wilhelm **Stekel's** only contributions to medical science been the enunciation of these propositions and their vigorous advocacy, he would deserve to have a statue erected in his honor by the liberated youth of the world."

So, in 70th of XX century we could find in the manuals for sexual intercourse the thesis according to which everything is good between spouses who loves each other. I still hesitate is it good for unmarried man and woman. Anyway minet is excused in the modern society.

Once upon a time in Kiev City at one of a shoe factory the very interesting story had happened. It was not minet in an oval cabinet but something like this.

The factory was supervised by young director who did not yet have a higher education diploma but had the strong protectors. Director was arrogant and impolite to his close subordinates who had human dignity and higher education diplomas. So they joined in a conspiracy.

During one of the director's inspection of the factory premises the conspirers gave heed to his close interest to one of the young woman-worker. Then they managed to transfer the woman into the building of factory administration, close to the director's office. It was real promotion because the woman has occupied a new position with an increased salary.

The woman was a real beauty in a Slavic style. Rounded splendid body emitted sexual fluids, then big plump lips, over medium height, and very attractive legs. Before long she was invited to the director's cabinet where the earth's miracle has happen.

The director and the woman began to meet in the cabinet behind the closed doors very often during the working hours. And then the second miracle has come - she became pregnant.

Russian proverb says "The appetite comes with eating." Young woman demanded director to divorce his wife and marry her. Director hesitated. The woman began to press him, called his wife several times. The director's wife in her turn made written request to the district Communist party committee: "Bring my husband back to the family!"

The end of the story was not happy to anybody. Director lost his position, was transferred to other, very small facility. His wife has suffered too because of the essential reduction of husband's salary. Young lady was forced to make an abortion and to leave the factory.

Then there was one more unexpected turn. It became known that the chief engineer of the factory had also a mistress, the factory's employee. So, he was forced to leave the factory too.

This woman was not a secretary. In Russia however the usual run of things - director's affair with a secretary.

<The loaders are taking away a divan from the director's office.

Woman-secretary: "What is going on? I am going to be fired?">

<There is a competition for a secretary position. Pretenders are asked: "How much is two by two?"

First woman answered: "Four".

Second woman: "Four and a half".

Third woman: "How much do you need?"

Here is the real event from life.

The secretary became pregnant. She demanded her lover-director to marry her. The director has refused.

The woman brought an action against the director to the court for paying an allowance due to a child from the father on desertion.

The director brought two witnesses, his friends, to the court who testified that they had sexual intercourse with the woman the same period of time as the director (the DNA paternity diagnostics did not yet exist).

The Judge ruled: "Each man must pay one third of the allowance due to the child on desertion."

Let's continue with the salty but witty anecdotes.

<A car stopped in the middle of the street. The owner is trying to repair the car but is not able to do any good.

He stops a car that coming by and asks its driver to help him.

The driver is trying his best but no way out.

He asks the owner of the car: "Do you have a secret?"

The owner looks at the driver with astonishment.

The driver repeats his question a couple of times.

At last the owner of the car is losing his self-control:

"Yes. I have a secret. I sleep with my mother-in-law. And you think this thing can help to start the engine?">

(Russian drivers call by "secret" a secret device in the car that prevents car from stealing).

<A child is going to be 16 years old.

A mother of the child asks his father to teach their son the basics of a sexual education.

The father keeps refusing not knowing what to say and especially how to say.

The wife patiently explains him:

"First tell him about a sexual life of butterflies, then birds and after that - how it happens with humans."

At last the father decides to try.

He calls the son and speaks to him:

"Remember, pal, how we had a sexual intercourse with our housemaid last year. So, the butterflies and the birds do this the same way.">

<Five-year old boy is boasting to his friends.

"Now we have all things at home."

The friends ask him to explain.

The boy says: "My father returned back from the business trip and brought a venereal disease. And my mother said that we did not have for now on only this thing.">

<Six years old boy had a wash in the women's department of public bathes which he visited together with his mother and grandmother.

(Long time ago, after the World War II, many of the soviet citizens did not have a hot water in their homes).

After visiting bathhouse the boy is sharing his impressions with his friends: "You will not trust me, guys. I saw one woman who had on the left thigh a tattoo of **Lenin**, on the right thigh a tattoo of **Stalin**, and in between, I think, a tattoo of Karl **Marx** because of a big thick beard.">

<A student is sleeping in a hostel.

All of a sudden he began to make movements as if he is winding something on his arm.

His neighbor awakened him asking what the matter.

The student: "I had a dream that in the house on the opposite side of the street a beautiful girl is undressing. My penis began to elongate, crawled out of the blanket, climbed on the window-sill, went down to the street, crossed the street-car rails, and began to clamber up the wall aiming the girl's window. And at this time I saw a street-car going by the street.">

At the end of the chapter let us laugh at soft anecdotes.

<Young married couple asks their physician:

"Doctor, what can we do that not to get pregnant?"

The physician answers: "You must drink Borzhomi[8]."

Happy couple is leaving. In some time they are returning.

"Doctor, we forgot to ask you, what time we need to drink Borzhomi: Before or after."

The doctor answers: "Instead of.">

<Young couple is dancing a slow dance being very close to each other and passionate.

Elder woman is standing by the door, watching. At last she could not contain herself:

"Poor kids! Why are you tormenting yourselves? You better lie down.">

---

8   Borzhomi – a Caucasian mineral water.

<Husband and wife are in the bed. Beyond the wall their close neighbors are placing new furniture.

The couple hears through the wall.

"Do just a little right - No - Do just a little left - Very good - Now, closer, closer - Excellent!'

Husband says to the wife: "Here is the real sex, not what we make!"

The author does not want to leave an impression that he is a vulgar old man who never valued the real love. Contrary, my most favorite songs are "The girl from Ipanema", "The shadow of your smile", most favorite movies "Snow falling on cedars", "The bridges of Madison county", the most favorite stories are Jack **London's** "The end of the story", "The serf of Kanaka", **Bunin's** "Sunstroke", "Shadowed paths".

However, a joke has a right for living reflecting the other side of the phenomena. It could be used by the person who was not happy to find a true romantic love. It is not so easy to obtain this gift of the Lord.

Madge, the heroine of "The end of the story" says: "No one can explain love, I least of all. I only knew love, the divine and irrefragable fact, that is all."

And at last the verse of the Russian prominent poet **Bryusov**.

MISTY NIGHTS
All in tears I'm standing by threshold
Of the door I have entered before,
And the letters of stars fuse in sorrowful lines.
Oh, misty haze nights in the blazing hot June!

There, right there on the closed dark terrace,
Kindled passionate eyes kept bowing me over,
Dear face lines disfigured in a vehement grimace.
Oh, misty haze nights! Oh, misty haze nights!

Here is the mystery of terrestrial pleasures...
Is it the thing I expected to find!
I'm shaking from shame - I am laughing!
You had lied me, shadows!
You had lied me haze misty June nights!

SOCIALISM AND COMMUNISM

"I pass the test that says a man who isn't a socialist at 20 has no heart, and a man who is a socialist at 40 has no head." (William **Casey**. Quoted in obituary, *Washington Post, May 7,1987*[9]).

AMNESTY
The man,
Who had shot my father in Kiev City
In summer of thirty eight
Is still alive.
Probably he left
In order a pension to get,
And lives in a peace
And business his habitual
Abandoned.
  Well, if he had died -
  Probably alive is the man
  Who before the very execution
  By thick
  Wire
  Twisted
  The hands
  Of my father
  Behind his back;

---

9 The saying has been attributed to French socialist politician and premier Aristide **Briand** (from **Andrews**, Robert; see in the *Literature*).

He apparently also
A pension had gotten.

But if he had died,
Then probably alive is the man
Who tortured my father
In inquests;
Apparently this one had gotten
A pretty good pension.
Maybe the convoy man
Who led my father
On the execution
Is still alive.
If I wish,
I could return
To my Motherland.
I heard
All these people
Forgave me.
(Russian poet Ivan **Elagin**
1918, Vladivostok, Russia – 1987, Pittsburgh, USA)

Many people all over the world continue to believe in the "bright future" - socialism and then - communism. They keep calling Karl **Marx** as a great scientist, the founder of a new "religion" for the labor people, the one who had "foretold" the historical inevitability of the crash of the capitalism and the building of the socialism and then the communism society.

The harbingers of the communism proclaimed that the "bright future" must have two stages: the socialism - everybody should work using own abilities to the full and receive a salary according to one's labor contribution; the communism - everybody should work using own abilities to the full and receive a salary according to one's necessities of life ("from each according to his ability, to each according to his need)."

There is one more form of the communism which was described by famous Russian writer **Nagibin**. In his short story (see the *Literature*) he described famous CPSU boss **Brezhnev** as the great communist who was placed by people's will into this bright paradise where all things in need are available without labor.

In 1961 the Communist Party of the Soviet Union announced the communism's coming: "Communist Party solemnly proclaims - present generation of the Soviet people will live in the communism."

It was said by **Khrushchev** who at the same time declared that the well-being of the soviet people is steadily rising. Then he advanced the slogan: "Let's overtake and surpass the USA!"

Soviet people at once commented these calls by anecdotes.

Regarding the communism:

<There is a conversation of two men.

"Pal, what do you think, shall we live up to the communism?"

"Surely we shall not. But I have a pity for our children.">

Regarding the USA:

<Probably we could overtake the USA, but we cannot surpass her, because the Americans would see our bare buttocks.>

Regarding the well-being of the Soviet people:

<One man asked riddle to the other man: "What is rising that we are not able to see?"

Other man promptly answered: "The level of the soviet people's well-being.">

The same thing is happening nowadays. Russian press is trying with all it might to depict an idyllic picture of the current life of the Russian people. It uses all means including the achievements in the soccer competition and in the art.

Once upon a time Russian poet **Yevtushenko** has written: "… and even in the field of a ballet we are at the front of a whole planet." The poet meant a classical ballet. Maybe he just forgot to mention that Russian classical ballet was founded completely by French ballet masters Jules **Perrot**, Arthur **Saint-Leon**, and Marius **Petipa**.

There is also a modern ballet too, where America stands at the front of a whole planet. However some intimate connection between American and Russian ballets surely exists. The modern ballet was founded by the great American dancer and ballet master Isadora **Dunkan** (who had dramatic Russian experience) and by the outstanding American choreographer of Russian origin George **Balanchine**.

Using the method of the famous Russian theatrical creator **Stanislavskiy** I would like to say: "I do not believe!" How could be such a Renaissance in the country with no real democracy, no real respect for private property, no real justice, in the country that visits her "friends" on tanks.

But let us look at the Soviet socialism.

In spite of the horrors of the French revolution, in spite of the millions corpses due to the Bolsheviks' overturn in 1917 in Russia, in spite of tortures and genocide in the Soviet Union, prisons and labor camps, the adherents of the socialism in Russia and in America too keep saying: "I believe. In the future we would build a 'good socialism, the socialism with a human face'."

It is interesting and useful to try to hear the wise voice from the past which in 1896 said firmly: "Socialism propagates itself in any manner rather than by reason. Feeble in the extreme when it attempts to reason, and to support itself by economic arguments, it becomes on the contrary extremely powerful when it remains in the region of dreams, affirmations, and chimerical promises..."

And what is much more important: "Let anyone read the declarations, full of hope and enthusiasm, issued by our Socialists of fifty years ago, at the moment of the revolution of 1848, of which they were the most valiant partisans. ... Thanks to them their country sank into a despotism; and, a few years later, into a formidable war and invasion. Scarcely half a century has passed since this phase of Socialism, and already forgetful of this latest lesson we are preparing ourselves to repeat the same round."

It was a voice of **Le Bon** about the socialism in general and socialism of the French revolution in particular. The voice had sounded in 1896 in his book *The Psychology of Socialism*.

Then we can receive the one more revelation from the person who got to know the Soviet socialism not by hearsay. This is the widow of the prominent Russian poet **Mandelstam**, who has been tortured and killed during the great Bolshevik's purge of the XX century. In her book *Hope* *against Hope* Nadezhda **Mandelshtam**, adduces the words of the young man, a witness of the socialism years in the USSR: "It is well known that everybody who has ever tried to make people happy only brought total disaster on them."

The first peculiarity of the Soviet socialism is cruelty; the same (maybe much bigger) as it was in the France 150 years ago. It was cruelty without any mercy and legal prosecution.

Soviet State had an excellent code of laws - Soviet Constitution. But in reality the Communist Party's bigwigs did what they wanted following the famous Russian proverb: "What I want, I do." But in a real life there were not just the foolish tricks.

Here are the two anecdotes.

<American archeologists in Egypt found the skeleton from the period of approximately 3,000 years ago. They were not able to determine whom those bones belong. French and British archeologists failed to do this too.

Then they called Soviet archeologists. Ten men in the black suits and American diagonal stripe ties arrived and locked themselves with the skeleton up in a secluded room.

They went out after three hours with suits and ties torn to pieces.

"It was **Amenemhat** [10]Third", the Soviets said.

"How did you manage to determine?" - Americans asked.

"He confessed by himself.">

<A camel has disappeared from a zoo. The chief of the police department was called by the top authorities and requested to find the animal. After three days the chief

---

10   This was the dynasty of Pharaohs (rulers) in the ancient Egypt.

reported that the camel was found, and zoo's employee can take him off from his office.

The journalists gathered in the office, and the chief ordered to bring the camel.

A policeman brought a cardboard box, took off a cover, and everybody saw that in the box a hare was sitting.

"But where is a camel?"- amazed journalists gasped.

The hare began to cry.

"I shall confess once more time that I am a camel, but do not beat me by the feet again.">

The second peculiarity of the Soviet socialism is an all-devouring fear: to be imprisoned without guilt, to tell an anecdote, to criticize authority, to make a mistake pronouncing or writing the name of a communist bigwig.

At the end of 30-th of the last century all soviet families lived in a constant fear. All nights long my mother and father could not sleep listening closely to the outside sounds. If it was the sound of a parking car, somebody in the building should be arrested.

At the end of 40th my father urgently took my mother off from the state job because of a danger to be accused of being a cosmopolitan[11]. Everybody, not only Jewish persons, had no right to have a positive attitude to the Western world, especially to the USA. This time we, schoolboys in the primary school, had excessive fear to use American fountain-pens or chewing-gums ("the symbols of the capitalism").

All the rest about the concentration camps in Siberia and the soviet prisons American people, I suppose, know good enough. The fear exists and now: to lose a job, to be condemned of something wrong without evidence.

---

11   See in the *Vocabulary*.

<A hare is running over the state border.

A frontier guard stops him:

"Why are you running?"

The hare is answering:

"I heard that they cut the testicles to the bears."

"But why you are running?"

The hare: "Look, they will catch me, will cut my testicles off, and then try to prove that you are not a bear.">

<A cab is going down the Moscow.

A taxi-driver says very quietly:

"We are passing the Red Square.[12]"

A passenger asks: "Why are you whispering?" Driver: "Yesterday I have drunk some cold beer.">

The soviet people knew one more kind of fear -to make an independent decision, action, to express opinion different from the official one. I think that now the same thing exists too, maybe not only in Russia and Ukraine.

<The English Queen gives a dinner party for the foreign diplomats.

All of a sudden she has hiccupped.

The French ambassador presents his apologies: "Pardon, messeurs, I have an increased acidity."

The dinner is continuing. The Queen utters a belching sound.

The Italian ambassador presents his apologies. "Scusi, seniore, I am not good to-day."

In some time the Queen utters a sound of winds letting out.

---

12   Red Square – see the *Vocabulary*.

The soviet ambassador darts off and ran out of the hall. Then he returns and says: "I have consulted with Moscow. This sound we take upon ourselves.">

<Somebody is calling by phone.
"Is this **Abramovich**?"
"No. This is the KGB"
This somebody is singing:
"*Unbreakable union of freedom republics...*[13]">

And also the soviet people knew the essential economical shortages. About the middle of 1970th they enjoyed the anecdote.

<There is a big national question: "How to manage economical shortages in the USSR?"
Answer: "It is necessary one month do not provide any help to the Cuba, one month do not drink at the working days, one month do not steal from the industrial plants.>

Once upon a time I was observing outside the big instrument-making plant during the lunch-hour the proceeding of the very long beer-queue. In Russian style the beer was served in the mugs poured from the big cistern. Many of the workers added good amount of vodka in the mug with a beer.

My friends had also very interesting observation. At the end of the working shift at the very big tannery the workers were leaving. Many of them were carrying the leather wrapped round their bodies under the clothes. Some of them who drank heavily at once after leaving the tannery were conveyed

---

13   This is the first line of the soviet anthem.

by the police to the sobering-up station and were forced to leave the leather to the authorities. One smart worker whose home was very close to the tannery has built a catapult and sent the parcels with leather straight to his wife.

OUR ADDRESS IS
THE SOVIET UNION ...

(this is the name of the soviet popular song)

Hammer on the right,
Sickle on the left,
This is our proud Soviet amulet.
You want - you strike,
You want - you reap.
Anyway you'll get a s - - t.

Everybody loves his own country, especially Motherland. Some people had left the one. Why?

Somebody left for freedom, somebody escaping the humiliation. Somebody just looking for the better living conditions, according to popular Russian saying "A fish is looking where is deeper, a man is looking where is better."

In 1948 Soviet poet **Mikhalkov** wrote the fable about the cosmopolitans. Here is a fragment from the fable.

I know, still the families exist
That smearing our own country things,
Delighted seeing foreign labels,
Keep eating Russian lard however.

Now, living in the USA, the author has met many emigrants from the former Soviet Union about which is possible to say vice versa.

I know, many emigrants exist

That smearing all American good things,

Unable to forget the history of Red,

So eager to receive free food and cheapest bed[14].

Many of them celebrate soviet holidays (Soviet Army day, October upheaval day), are the fans of Russian sportsmen, teams, celebrate together with Russian newspapers in America the anniversaries of "heroes" who caused damage to the USA (for example, of ones who helped to steal USA secrets of the atomic bomb on behalf of the USSR).

In the former Soviet Union, now in Russia there is one so popular conception: "We are the best everywhere every time. Most of all inventions and discoveries, other great things of all times were done first by the Russians."

No doubt Russians are the very great people. The world knows many prominent Russian scientists, artists, writers, musicians, poets, inventors, sportsmen.

But too much is too much! It is necessary to respect the other cultures.

Communist party of the Soviet Union used to prepare the slogans to the soviet holidays. The anti-soviet people used to invent the modified ones:

<The soviet paralysis is the most progressive paralysis in the whole world!>

<The soviet microelement is the biggest microelement in the whole world!>

---

14   Food stamps and section 8 Housing program.

< If there is no food-lines we would created the ones.>

<"Steelmakers, your strength is in your plavki .">
(In Russian language one word 'plavki' is used both for 'fusions' and for 'swimming trunks').

Russian Tsar Peter I, the Great dreamed to extend Russia to the warm seas. Many of his successors, including soviet governments, did not abandon this plan. However in the contemporary world it is becoming more and more difficult to realize this kind of plan by a military power. So, a "quiet expansion" is in action.

In 1975 together with my friends I had a rest in the famous Ukrainian resort of Yalta. The best beaches were closed for the soviet people who did not have a voucher for a rest house or a sanatorium. This time there were many tourists from the German Democratic Republic (see: GDR in the *Vocabulary)*. And one my friend, who had the very strong anti-soviet feelings, used to say: "The Germans were not able to defeat us during the World War II, but now they have easily occupied our best beaches."

The quiet expansion continues in our time. The best example is the Great Britain.

Nobody can say that all people in the Communist countries hated the authorities. How many of them? I do not know, but suppose that a lot. I can only speak on behalf of those who did hated or despised the soviet reality.

Here is one more anecdote about **Khrushchev.**

<In 1953 right after **Khrushchev** was elected by the general secretary of the CPSU, one person called him 'a fool' and was condemned to 18.5 years in prison. What for?

It was half year for insult of personality, 18 years for divulgence of a state secret.>

The regime haters did not spare anybody including big shots in the scientific world. By the way, many of the "Soviet scientific leaders" did not have enough scientific weight to supervise scientists. For example, among the directors of the Ukrainian psychological institute at Kiev-City one director was the former Komsomol leader, second - the former Communist Party leader, the head of the department in the technical university (the name of the department was 'The history of the CPSU').

<The action is occurring in the Kremlin palace at the time of the Congress of best workers and peasants of the Soviet Union.

Ivan and Maria (female) from the solitude villages are sitting on the far gallery and looking at the presidium of the Congress.

Ivan to Maria: "Maria, do you want me to show you **Keldysh**[15]?"

Maria (becoming confused, turning red):

"Are you crazy? You will show me it in the hotel-room.">

Maybe the most popular anti-soviet anecdotes are about **Chapayev**, the hero of the Russian Civil War, his lieutenant Piet'ka (short name for Peter) and female machine-gunner Anka (short name for Anna).

In 1934 the very talented movie about **Chapaev** was shot. I was delighted by this action movie in my childhood like many of my schoolmates. And then, all of a sudden (about 1962) many anecdotes about **Chapayev** made their appearance,

---

15   The name of the famous scientist (see: *the Name Directory*).

and continued to multiply like an avalanche. Some of them are cruel, some - inoffensive, most - very witty.

<Private is running into the headquarters and saying:

"Comrade **Chapaev**, on the roof Piet'ka is stretching the aerial."

Chapaev: "Look! What the curious names people can contrive."

(In Russian language the word 'to stretch' has two meanings: 1) stretching of something, 2) to have a sexual intercourse with a woman).>

<Private is saying: "Comrade **Chapaev**, in our village the Fantomas[16] has slept with all women."

Chapaev smugly twisting his moustache:

"Was it really Fantomas!?">

<**Chapaev** has made an attempt to pass the entrance exams to the Military Academy. When he returned to the unit Piet'ka asked him:

"So what, comrade Chapaev, did you pass?"

"No, Piet'ka. I gave up the analyses of urine, of excrement, but failed in mathematics."

(In Russian language there is one world for passing an exam and to submit, give up something).>

<In a primary school it is going to be a patriotic party in the memory of Russian Civil War heroes.

Vova (short name for Vladimir) has bragged that his grandfather saw **Chapaev**-hero alive.

So, Vova's grandfather was invited to the party.

---

16 'Fantomas' –is the very popular French movie about diabolic protagonist 'Fantomas' with superstars Jean **Marais** and Louis de **Funes**.

The grandfather is telling: "We are sitting in the ambush on the bank of Ural River[17]. All of a sudden I saw **Chapaev** who was swimming across the river. I took an aim on my rifle, shut, and had never seen him again.">

<Piet'ka: "Comrade **Chapaev**, you are an oak!"
Chapaev: "You are right, Piet'ka. I am very strong."
(In Russian language the word 'an oak' has a double meaning: big tree and a stupid person).>

<**Chapaev** is flying on a dashing horse leading the cavalry charge against the enemies from the White Army forces.

All of a sudden he sees Anka who cannot fire from her machine gun that became wedged.

Chapaev is shouting: "Anka, once again it happens and I would f--k you up!"

Anka: "Comrade **Chapaev**, how many times you just keep promising!"(In Russian language the words 'to f--k up' have two meanings: 1) the usual, 2) to punish somebody).>

The beginning of the Soviet anthem has been already mentioned in the book. It is so picturesque that it is worth to repeat it one more time: *Unbreakable union of freedom republics.*

Many nations which in other circumstances could be friendly to the Russian people being united in the Soviet Union by the brutal Bolsheviks' force became so much hostile to the Soviet realities. Especially this is true regarding Baltic countries (Latvia, Lithuania, Estonia), Ukraine and Georgia. The last events in Georgia (in August 2008) showed that Russia is not going to stop its expansion and brutality.

---

17   This is the river between the European and Asian parts of the Russia.

The author lived long time in the Ukraine, knew many real Ukrainians who valued so much their native language and native culture. By the way, the Ukrainian language is very poetic, melodious. Ukrainians whom author knew never wanted to make controversy with Russians. They just wanted to have their own independent state.

It is astonishing that the author is unable to remember any anecdotes (except of one) regarding national relations in the former USSR. May be these anecdotes did not exist in a big amount. The same thing you can say about the book of Ben Lewis. Why? I do not know.

I remember only one anecdote on this topic.

<Once upon a time the USSR had in its structure the Karelian[18]-Finnish Soviet Socialist Republic.

Then the Government decided to rename Karelian-Finnish Soviet Socialist Republic into Karelian Autonomous Soviet Socialist Republic (lower rank in former Soviet Union structure). Why?

Because of during the check-up it turned out that in the Karelian-Finnish Soviet Socialist Republic there were only two Finns: Finn-inspector (IRS financial inspector) and **Finkelshteyn**.

During the next, more thorough check-up, it revealed that there is the only one Finn in the Republic , because Finn-inspector and **Finkelshteyn** were the same person.>

The next issue is probably the most prominent and shocking topic of the Soviet life: restricted moving from one place to another.

---

18   Karelian – belongs to Karelia, the region in the north Russia.

The peasants did not have the passports. So they had to get the ones to move to a city. To live in a city all Soviet citizens must had the residential permit (so-called 'propiska' - registration of a passport, the right for permanent residence in the concrete city, town). As far as I know nothing has changed for now. 'Propiska' is still alive. I can say that this creature is the one of the biggest achievement of the Soviet Socialism's system in depraving its citizens.

For an ordinary soviet citizen the travelling abroad, even in the country that belonged to the socialistic camp was a heaviest trick. The person must have a positive reference from the local Communist Party organization, and to pass a check-up in the KGB.

After Perestroyka the ordinary citizen did not have to pass the check-up in the KGB but could not afford the skyrocketing prices for plane tickets.

In the sixtieth of the last century I have a good acquaintance. His nickname was 'an American' because of he always was dressed only in the garments and shoes "made in USA". He was a black-marketeer (in Russian language "fartsovshchik") - used to buy the clothes from the USA and most developed European countries tourists and sold them for the higher price to the soviet people. For this activity he was imprisoned for five years behaving very decent during the trial and in the jail.

When the time of free moving abroad came he could only look sadly at the departing people. The prison broke down his health. I think that he is the one who deserve to live in the USA much more than many other immigrants.

<One soviet citizen asks the other:

"Man, what are you going to do when the soviet frontiers would be open?"

"I shall climb on the tree."

"Why?"

"I shall be trampled under feet.">

<Soviet citizen came to the KGB and asks to give him permission to move to the USA where he is going to provide a permanent care for his uncle who lost his hearing.

KGB officer replies him.

"I have a better proposition for you. Let your uncle move to the Soviet Union, where you will be able to care of him for your best."

The citizen answers: "You did not understand me. My uncle lost his hearing, not brains.">

<Soviet citizen is trying imperceptibly to get over the soviet frontier.

Frontier guard noticed him.

"Stop immediately! Where are you going?"

The man has squatted and pretended that he is defecating.

Frontier guard came closer.

"What are you doing here?"

The man rose to his feet: "Don't you see?"

Frontier guard looked down.

"But this is a dog's shit."

"C'est la Vie[19]," - the man answered.>

When some of the Soviet citizen was lucky to have official journey to a foreign country he was under permanent surveillance.

---

19   In French: "Such is the life."

My good acquaintance from the Kiev-City Opera and Ballet Theatre told me that during the foreign tours many KGB agents were included in the troupe disguised under administrators or stage workers.

My friend from the famous Ukrainian National Folk Dance Ensemble named by **Virskiy** told me about the very strict rules for troupe members during the foreign tours: no contacts with the citizens of a foreign country, no outside sexual intercourse.

<A big Soviet merchant vessel came to the South foreign port.

The sailors went out onto the decks.

Many prostitutes gathered beside the vessel and began to invite the sailors down.

The sailors keep silence.

The prostitutes began to make guesses which could explain sailors' denials.

"Are you impotents?"

No answer.

"Are you homosexuals?"

No answer again.

"Are you masturbators?"

Embarrassed sailors keep silence.

"Oh, you are soviets!" the prostitutes guessed at last.>

The anti-Semitism is well-known topic, not only for Soviet Union and Russia. In Soviet Union the anti-Semitism was both on the state and the commonplace level. This is nothing new.

<Election of a Trade Union boss is in action in the outside world.

Election committee members lead discussion regarding the candidates.

They appeal to an elder man with a big beard who is sitting quietly in the distance reading a big volume.

"Why you do not want to be a Trade Union boss?"

The old man responds:

"I cannot be elected on this important post."

"Why?"

"First of all I am not a member of the Trade Union.

Second: I am not a member of the Communist Party.

And at last: I am a Jew."

"And what is your name?"

"Karl **Marx**.">

<Soviet citizen came to the human resources department looking for a job. The supervisor asks him: "Who are you?"

"I am a designer,"- the citizen is answering proudly.

"I see that you are not **Ivanov**[20]. I ask about your profession.">

Maybe for American reader would be interesting to know that usually the supervisor of the human resources department was former KGB employee.

And at the end of this part of the book I would like to talk about the life of the soviet intelligent.

The first distinguished feature - very low salary. Real intelligent who did not steal from the state was very poor. The technical engineers, the school-teachers had the lowest salary in the USSR.

---

20   Last name **Ivanov** means that the nationality of the person is Russian, not Jewish.

Then the next important feature. An intelligent in the Soviet Union was treated as a second sort of man after the workers and peasants due to the mentality of the leaders of 1917 October upheaval.

For example, the University associate professor could hear from his wife: "You are not a real male. It is not enough that your salary is much lower than our neighbor gets, who is just a manager of supplies; you are not able to hold a hummer in your hands to hummer a nail."

And the last not the least point. Soviet bigwigs had much lower mental capacities in comparison with the real intelligent, permanently lied to get high position and were very greedy. It is easy to understand how difficult, having an inferiority complex, to accept somebody who is mentally higher. And from the other hand, it is easy to imagine the sufferings of the real soviet intelligent, the humiliation he was exposed.

Here is the poem in prose regarding the soviet intelligent.

ONE DAY IN THE LIFE OF SOVIET INTELLIGENT

The stones began to fall down with a heavy crash. The flock of chamois clambered up the rocks. One chamois stumbled and began to slip slowly down. The body covered by short fur kept squeezing the chest. The sun was scorching, there was not enough air.

A thin beam of life penetrated up from the depths of the brain. Dream phantoms were stepping back. **Konstantinov** lied on his belly bathed in sweat.

"What the time?" he thought in fright, and forced himself to turn his body on the back, trying to sit up. It was not so easy.

"At last, you are awaked, alcoholic!" it was a voice of his wife.

Konstantinov did not answer. He managed to hold a sitting position, now trying to stand up. Inside him something was constantly dropping off, he was staggering.

"I hardly dragged you home yesterday night,"- he heard the wife's voice again.

Now **Konstantinov** was threading his way to the kitchen, to the refrigerator where according to his calculations should be a bottle of a mineral water.

At the kitchen table his wife was hurriedly finishing her breakfast.

"Give me, a double coffee, please, I do not want to eat,"- **Konstantinov** growled out.

"May be you would like a triple coffee,"- the wife snarled. "How long ago you used to bring home coffee, breadwinner."

Konstantinov said nothing and left to work.

In the laboratory sitting by his desk **Konstantinov** understood that his decision to deny breakfast was a thoughtless one. He was tormented by a weakness, felt sick and was not able to concentrate.

"Vadim Vadimych, it looks like you are out of a good conditions today,"- observed Nina Nikolayevna[21], the engineer from his design group.

"Yes, I have relaxed myself yesterday," **Konsrantinov** attempted to smile, but his face muscles failed to obey him. "We celebrated the defense of the dissertation[22]..."

---

21 Vadim Vadimych – the first and patronymic names of **Konstantinov**.
    Nina Nikolayevna – first and patronymic names of this female-engineer.

22 Dissertation – see: the *Vocabulary*.

"I understand, the event is momentous," Nina Nikolayevna sighed and looked at Allochka, the young drafts-woman. "Will your husband also be a candidate soon?"

"Maybe he will," Allochka[23] answered reluctantly. "What is the good of it?"

Konstantinov has deepened in his thoughts. At the banquet table of one of the most fashionable restaurant was noisy. The young scientists argued about a rightfulness of a negative result in scientific research. **Konstantinov** declared himself as an opponent.

Now he was arguing in his thoughts again. "The result cannot be negative," **Konstantinov** was thinking. " The result is something that has been done, something that has concrete final expression. And negative - this is something that does not exist..."

"**Konstantinov**, the Chief is calling for you,"- leading engineer from the co-operating technical group interrupted the dense flow of his thoughts.

The Chief casted a cursory glance at **Konstantinov** and showed him by a gesture to take a seat.

"Listen, Vadim Vadimych, you have proposed an interesting construction, but it is necessary to carry it out. Your group is hopelessly late. What can you say for your excuse?"

"But we are working, Petr Stepanovich[24]," **Konstantinov** began vigorously, "we are looking for the different ways of realization, turning down non-constructive, non-elegant solutions..."

---

23   Allochka – the diminutive tender female name for Alla.

24   Petr Stepanovich – first and patronymic names of the Chief.

"Do not use the fine words, Vadimych,"- the Chief has interrupted him. "You are not in the research institute. You must make production, fulfill the plan."

"However sometimes is not bad to think a little."

"Think but do your part in time," cut the Chief short. "Watch your people, smoke less with Nina Nikolayevna..."

All of a sudden the Chief noticed **Konstantinov**'s sore face.

"Did you take an offence?" he asked.

"And I have no right to take an offence?"

Now the Chief was examining attentively **Konstantinov**'s face.

"Oh, I did understand at last," he burst into laughter."You have distinguished yourself at the banquet table, got completely drunk yourself yesterday. How was the dissertation?"

"The dissertation was very interesting,"- **Konstantinov** has livened up. "Somebody proposed even to recommend it for a doctor's degree. There was discussion, controversy..."

"O.K., Vadim Vadimych,"- the Chief has summed up. - "Go home, come to yourself, but to-morrow begin to work appropriately."

Konstantinov does not want to go home. He decided to have a bite, to calm himself and first of all to drink a coffee.

His joyful expectation has been destroyed at the very first attempt.

In front of the entrance to the empty hall of the respectable restaurant he was resolutely stopped by young administrator in an expensive suit and with a big golden signet-ring.

"We have a special service today, comrade," the administrator politely barred the way taking a glance of the appraisal over **Konstantinov**. "Did not you see the notice?"

Crushed both by this killing argument and the appearance of its owner **Konstantinov** immediately has sunk and left the restaurant. Going out he saw the notice and recollected that he uses to see the one any time he passes by.

"No problem," he tried to cheer himself. Lunch in this place costs a weekly salary."

His mood had a little bit risen, and he vigorously began to stroll down the street.

At the next trade outlets he saw the notices "We have no water", "We have no coffee", "The sanitary hour." Inclined to scientific thinking **Konstantinov** made a conclusion: "Do not try to drink coffee in the time interval between one hour before lunch and one hour after lunch of trade outlet." Then suddenly he gained an insight into the problem: "I have got a negative result in my research!"

At a grocery store he drank a glass of tomato juice and ate a bit of biscuit.

Now he was beside a movie house where a new film was demonstrated. The name of the film was "A little Vera[25]". It was the first Soviet movie with a sexual intercourse on the screen.

Konstantinov came out from the movie house being completely depressed. Being long time married, **Konstantinov** never knew about such whimsicality in sex. "Sure!" he recalled the popular saying, "There is no sex in the Soviet Union."

Now it was time to go home.

---

25   Vera – this is the female first name (in English means 'faith').

Konstantinov has squeezed himself into the overcrowded bus. The bus could be very comfortable unless being overcrowded and having very narrow exit passage at the front door. The workers of a bus depot essentially extended the driver's place using the rough metal sheets. Trying to exit **Konstantinov** anyway continued his scientific reasoning: "According to the theory of a 'local egoism' to make a comfort for a bus driver at the expense of the passengers."

At this moment the front door has been opened, an impatient crowd carried **Konstantinov** through the narrow passage, torn his pants that hooked the sharp edge of the metal sheet, and have thrown him out in the street.

The wife was already at home, and lay on a sofa reading a book. She did not even look at him.

Konstantinov tried to mend his pants, but following some inner unconscious impulse has left the apartment.

On the staircase **Konstantinov** met his young neighbor from the same floor.

"Vadim Vadimych, why are you so sad?" the neighbor nicely smiling opened the door of his apartment. "Come on in, relax."

In the apartment **Konstantinov** took off his shoes and came in the room trying not to swing the air. He saw expensive furniture, oriental carpets, painting. There was the typical apartment of a new bourgeois.

In the room **Konstantinov** saw one more guest, young sturdily-built male in expensive jeans suit.

The host proposed to play a preference[26]. The company made itself comfortable at the round card-table.

---

26   Card game *a Preference* is very popular game among University students and

From the beginning **Konstantinov** did not have a good hand. He has played a couple of ordinary games, took one trick on "miser".

"Jane, bring us something to get a bite,"- ordered the host.

Soon the host's wife appeared rolling small cart loaded with china coffee-pot, caviar sandwiches and the bottle of "Metaxa". By the smell **Konstantinov** understood that a coffee is coming.

He had on his hands four senior diamonds, aces, kings and queens in clubs and spade. Lead was not his.

"Nine diamonds"- **Konstantinov** secured himself.

From two other players' hands small trumps killed his aces and kings. He did not collect as a result three necessary tricks.

"Well, really!" the words escaped **Konstantinov**'s lips.

"Sometimes more serious event can be happened," the host assuaged him.

They drank coffee with brandy, have gotten a bite. **Konstantinov** tried to concentrate himself to finish the game not to be in a big loss.

"You owe one hundred fifty three rubles ," the host has announced the sentence for **Konstantinov**.

The wife was already in the bed reading the same book.

"Have you drunk a coffee?" she asked melancholically.

"How you have poured, exactly the same way I have drunk,"- **Konstantinov** snarled.

"Wait a moment!" the wife pricked her ears up. "Where have you been?"

---

intelligent.

"Where I have been - now I am not there,"- **Konstantinov** cut off.

The wife has drawn an air. She smelled the odor of expensive brandy, of American cigarettes.

"So you have visited our neighbor," she stated. "And how much have you lost?"

"It's none of your business,"- **Konstantinov** roared.

"Look! Here it is the negative result, you, the utter fool!" the wife said and continued to read.

A night-lamp shined cozy.

Konstantinov took a big folio and during the long time was examining on the first page a picture of an old man with clever eyes.

The bears were cycling, the monkeys - laughing, a hare blew the trumpet.

The book dropped out of his hands.

Konstantinov was sleeping.

SOVIET JEWS

The pianist M.R. told the following story: "It must have been in the seventies when my father and I met **Freud**-senior one day in the street. At the moment, I was arguing with my father about something. **Freud**-senior laughingly reproved me: 'What, do you contradict your father? My Sigmund's little toe is cleverer than my head, but he would never dare to contradict me!'" (from the book of Fritz **Wittels**).

Sigmund **Freud** was the greatest scientist between ever living giants. The second place I give to the Albert **Einstein**, the third - to the Norman **Wiener**. All of them were Jews.

I need this preamble because the Jews are very touchy. The years of anti-Semitism caused this state of affairs. I bear all my respect to this nation which my great grandparents killed during the Jewish pogrom belonged.

Here is the one of the best anecdote about the Jewish giant.

<Two Jews are talking.

The first: "Listen, who is **Einstein**?"

The second: "Albert **Einstein** is the outstanding scientist known all over the world."

The first: "Why he is so famous?"

The second: "Albert **Einstein** created the theory of relativity. Now he is going to Japan to be awarded by the Nobel prize for science."

The first: "What is the theory of relativity stands for?"

The second: "It is very difficult to explain."

The first: "Just try."

The second: "Imagine that you are having time with a lovely young woman. So, one hour seems to be for you like one second.

However if you are with your wife then one second seems to be for you like an hour."

The first (astonished): "Listen. You think it is worth to go to the Japan[27] just because of this khokhma[28] "?>

The next are the anti-soviet anecdotes.

< Abram: "Isaac, did you make a subscription for a newspaper?"

(In the Soviet Union everybody was obliged to subscribe for one of the Communist Party newspaper).

Isaac: "Why I need a newspaper if I have a radio-set?"

Abram: "Crazy-man, do you go to a lavatory with an aerial.">

<"**Abramovich**, have you stepped into the CPSU?"

Abramovich smells the air, lifts his foot.

"Do you think it stinks?"

(The word "to step into" has two meanings in Russia: 1) to join an organization, 2) to step on something).>

<Sam has invented a money printing machine.

A financial inspector from IRS has heard about this and has taxed him.

---

27   Albert **Einstein** received the Nobel Prize for the theory of photo-effect at Japan during World War II, but many people know him first of all for the theory of relativity.

28   Khokhma –this is a joke in Yiddish language.

Sam has paid.

The financial inspector increased the taxation.

Sam has paid again.

The financial inspector increased the taxation again.

Sam has brought the machine to the financial inspector and said:

"So now, print money by yourself and pay taxation by yourself too.">

<**Rabinovich's** parrot has flown away.

Rabinovich came to the KGB and said:

"If my parrot flies into your office, you must know that I do not share his opinions.">

Then the anecdotes about Jewish women are coming.

<Luke, why are you standing in the line with a night pot?

My Sarah said that they are giving some trash. (In Soviet slang the word "to give" has also the meaning to sell scarce products).>

<Abram went to a dentist.

He had bad toothache and kept holding his jaw by hands.

So the dentist was not able to do any procedure.

All of a sudden the dentist made an injection into Abram's buttocks.

Abram grasped his buttocks by hands, and dentist at last has got an access to the tooth.

At home Abram proudly tells his wife: "You know, Sarah, I have so deep roots that the dentist was forced to make shot in my buttocks."

The wife answers: "Now I understand why the smell from your mouth is like the one from your butt.">

The majority of Jewish anecdotes are about a good nature of the ordinary Jew: optimism, quick wit, wisdom, practicality, patience.

So, now I would like to propose the best anecdote from the best ones.

<"Marcus, could you buy 'Volga' "?

"Of course I can. However what for? I do not need so much water.">

('Volga' is the model of the famous Russian car and the name of the greatest Russian river).

There is also a very nice anecdote.

<Two Jews have met in London.

The first one asks the second one: "How do you do?"

"So-so,"- the second answers. "My wife betrays me with a Lord."

"And what is then?" the first asks.

"Two children," the second answers.

"Not bad. And what is your reaction?" the first asks.

"I have an affair with the Lord's wife," the second answers.

"It is better," the first encourages. "But why you are so sad, so sorrowful?"

"Because I make him Lords, and he makes me Jews.">

The anecdotes at the end of the chapter are exclusively about the Jewish wit.

<Isaac is walking to and fro a prison cell.

Cellmate: "Listen, pal, you think that if you are walking so you are not sitting".>(Russian language has one more meaning for 'to sit': 'to be in jail).

<Two Jews have met. One asks the other:
"How do you live? How do you can?"
Second: "I live but I cannot."
First: "Is it badly turns out?"
Second: "No. It turns out good. It's badly runs in.">

<Guest in the Solomon's home:
"Listen, Sol, your home looks like a bardack[29]."
Solomon: "O, thank you. Now I know where I forgot my galoshes.">

<What the difference between English man and Jewish man?
Englishman leaves without saying 'Good bye'. Jewish man keeps saying 'Good bye' and does not leave.>

---

29   This word has two meanings in Russian language: a prostitution house and untidiness.

USSR AND USA

VOLTAIRE: "I disapprove of what you say, but I will defend to the death your right to say it."

SAYING: God helps those who help themselves.

NIETZSCHE: "No," answered Zarathustra. "I give no alms. For that I am not poor enough." (*Thus Spoke Zarathustra. A Book for All and No*ne).

MICHALKOV:

Some were sitting on the bench,
Some were looking at the street,
Tolya sang, kept silence Boris,
Nikolay[30] kept swinging legs.

> Daw perched on nearest fence,
> Tomcat climbed on garret.
> Here said to children Boris
> Just to say:

I have nail in my pocket.
What you have?

> We'll have guest to-morrow coming.
> What you have?

We have gas in our kitchen.
What you have?

> We can see from our window

---

30   Tolya, Nikolay, Boris – male first names.

Red Square[31] *place.*
You can see from your window
Just a little bit of street.
(From the verse for children *And what do you have?*)

All these expressions are about USA, the verse - about the USSR, now - the Russia.

Russians and Americans are two great nations, the representatives of two great countries. Is their confrontation really necessary? Let us try to understand an answer on this question by the comparative analysis.

Respect of personality. Only American can be aware of being respected no matter of age.

Freedom of speech. Only American can be aware that he has an opportunity to criticize anybody not being persecuted (jailed or losing the job). Only he knows for a sure that there are influential persons in the Country who are ready to follow Voltaire.

Here is the anecdote.

<Russian and American men had an argument in whose country Freedom of speech is real.

American said:

"In my country everybody can come up to the White House and to shout 'the President is a fool!' "

Russian: "Well, is it the trick?

Every Russian can come up to the Kremlin and to shout 'the American President is a fool!' ">

---

31   Red Square – see: the *Vocabulary.*

American person works hard. He believes in God but know for a sure that he is the only one who must earn prosperity for his family.

In the scientific study of job satisfaction on an automobile assembly line of one of the big American plant **Walker** and **Guest** asked the assembly line workers

"What does your wife think of your job at the plant?"

The typical answers were: "She's glad I have a good-paying job and steady", "She likes the money and security. It enabled us to get married", "She likes it all right - PAY!" (pp. 88-89).

The work on the automobile assembly line was hard enough in the past. But it is very good to have a salary which makes a man able to keep his family well. Now many bored and monotonous operations on the assembly lines are made by robots. On the other hand, there are many people who perform repetitive operations many years completely satisfied by their work.

The author being a refugee from the former USSR began his labor history in the USA as a porter in a big liqueur store. It was necessary to feed the family and to teach the real American language.

The most excited part of the everyday's work was lavatories' cleaning, loading and unloading the heavy objects. So what?

I had several friends amongst co-workers. One of them was a very handsome man, tall, over 65, the veteran of the USA military forces. He had retirement benefits, had in the store a full-time job and during the week-ends worked as a valet parking employee. What for? For better support his grandchildren. All the rest of my life I shall admire this American man, the real representative of the Great country.

The opposite thing you could find in the USSR. People who performed hard works had a very low pay, and the most of the workers and employee received a very low salary. Even some who had comparatively higher salary were dissatisfied because they supposed fairly enough that for their skilled labor they should receive much higher salary. Here are two statements from the real persons.

<Former professional hockey-player, now the college teacher: "You say I work neither good nor bad! Look! How they pay me - the same way I work for them.">

<Professional soccer player during the team meeting regarding an increase the effectiveness of team efforts: "We have no premiums. You want us play for 'Thank you'. But: we are not able to put the 'Thank you' in a pocket, cannot pour the 'Thank you' in a glass.">

American government can repeat the words of **Nietzsche** about the alms. The government does not enforce people with very low income to beg providing a huge amount of Federal and State benefits. The benefits stretch from an unemployment compensation, Medicaid, Medicare, food stamps through the homemakers services with a pay to the relatives who provide the service. And there is also a Section 8 program, where in many cases the state actually pays mortgage to children of adult family members with the program.

But we can hear a lot of complaints. Many people suppose that money in the USA is growing on the trees. Probably the new Administration could consider this opportunity to increase sufficiently the level of wellbeing.

I can imagine a teenager who is standing by a glass window beside a big automobile luxury store. He is from family that is not wealthy, however he has desires as all human beings can have. He would like to be the owner of a luxury car as some of his schoolmates from the rich families.

What the feelings and intentions of this teenager? It depends upon his personality. But anyway in this situation of frustration he needs to use the mechanisms of the psychological defense which are the unconscious mental well doers serving to protect the personality against the danger that arises from negative feelings of dissatisfaction and frustration.

One person can use the mechanism of the rationalization. His train of thoughts might be: "I do not need this 'Jaguar'. Too much luxury, when at the same time the 'Ford' is not less reliable."

The other person can use the mechanism of compensation: "I am not able to be a writer or a lawyer who earn a lot of money to buy this 'Jaguar'. But I shall try my best to become a car racer, will earn enough money, and the car would be mine."

Sometimes a mechanism of overcompensation can be put into the action: "I would like to be a famous athlete. My physician supposes that I am restricted in my physical abilities due to a joint disease I had in my childhood. But now I am healthy and strong, I must work hard, I must overcome and make this accomplishment."

The next option for a frustrated person may be the mechanism of projection – unconscious ascribing own feelings onto others and acting toward them on the base of this perception: "I failed many things. I know for a sure that all my failures are due to these big fat cats who hate pour people blocking their way to the success."

And the last option for frustrated person is the delusional projection – unconscious ascribing own pathological (often paranoid) feelings onto others and acting toward them on the base of this perception: "Wait a little. I shall gain my strength and destroy all of you."

It is not so difficult to find the historical examples. Hitler before 1937 could be characterized by compensation, after 1937 - by delusional projection (see the book of John **Toland**). **Lenin** and **Stalin** all the ways long - by delusional projection.

Herbert **Wells** had met **Lenin** in 1920. Later he cited from one of **Lenin**'s work: "Those who took upon themselves the gigantic work of capitalism's annihilation, must realize, that they will be forced to try one method of action after another until at last they will find the one which mostly correspond theirs goals and tasks." And the main goal as **Lenin** said in his speech in 1919 is the "birth of the world federative soviet republic..." (From the book of **Latyshev**, pp.174-175).

Today I can only say: "God save America!"

Bolsheviks are bursting with envy (inferiority complex[32]) cultivated a hate to the inaccessible America. "What do you have? - What do we have?" This childish and at the same time sacramental question is unfortunately inherent to the mentality of soviet bigwigs.

Paid journalists all over the world hate the USA. Who paid them? It is so obvious; but many decent people are ashamed to pronounce the truth. Like in the well-know fairy tale of Hans Christian **Andersen** "The Emperor's New Clothes."

Let us return to the anecdotes.

---

32 Inferiority complex – the feeling to be inferior to the others in some way (more detailed description see in the *Vocabulary*).

<The American tourists are visiting a big train station in Moscow.

Guide-man tells: "This is the one of the biggest train-station in the world. Every 10 minutes a train arrives or departures."

One of the tourists says: "Excuse me, sir, we are here more than 15 minutes, and did not see any train coming or leaving."

The guide-man replies: "But in your America the blacks are discriminated.">

Many Russian people just pretend having negative feelings toward America being afraid of the authority. In their close circle they tell the anecdotes like this one.

<John **Kennedy** and Nikita **Khrushchev** had an argument, in which country alcoholism is higher. They made arrangement: to shoot any drunkard who is sleeping on the street.

They went down the Moscow, and Kennedy began to shoot without a break.

Then they came to the Washington.

Khrushchev went a long time with a loaded gun but in vain: no drunkards. At last he has noticed a sleeping drunk man, livened up his gun and shot.

It turned out to be the USSR ambassador in the USA.>

Many soviet people did not believe the anti-American importunate propaganda.

<Soviet citizen came to the 'KGB' and is asking:

"Give me, please, a permission to move to the USA."

The KGB's officer answers him using very popular Russian saying:

"It is good where we are absent. Why do you want to go to the USA?">

The citizen: "Because I would like to go where you are absent."

The authority and media cultivate the hate on the state level.

<Two crows are sitting nearby USA space-vehicle launching site. The "Challenger" is going to start.

USA crow: "It will fly up!"

USSR crow: "It will not fly up!"

Start was done and after a couple of seconds there is an explosion in the air.

USA crow: "You have evoked evil by your evil prophecies."

USSR crow: "I serve for the Soviet Union!">

America! America! For somebody she is a symbol of Freedom and Prosperity. For somebody - the catalyst of rage, hate, envy.

There is a popular Russian saying when something negative has happened in the family: "Who is guilty? You are right: daughter-in-law."

The same thing is happening when somebody without good intentions is talking about America. "Who is guilty for miniskirt? Who is guilty for AIDS[33]? Who is guilty for the crisis? Of course, the USA is guilty."

---

33 AIDS – Acquired Immunodeficiency Syndrome.

Last century at the end of 80-th the first channel of the soviet TV had a very popular evening program by the name of "Vzglyad" (in English - a Glance"). The program was managed by the former Komsomol functionaries.

One evening the young lovely lady-journalist who recently returned from a business trip to the USA took part in this program. The lady was telling about sexual education in the American primary schools. She told with a great enthusiasm that children about eight-nine years old receive during school lessons an education regarding the AIDS and how to prevent the one, using a condom (she called this device respectfully "Mister Condom").

The author of this book does not believe in many horrors that journalists ascribe to this monster and is very close not to believe in the very existence of such a disease at all, but was completely shocked by the age of the children and felt indignant to hear the next negative mention of the USA.

The result was the verse named *Bodiaga*[34].

BODIAGA
Once after "Vzglyad" programme gone
I have been killed by 'Mister Condom[35].'
I cannot sleep this night at all
Because American up-roar.
    What fellow-poor is baby Tom
    Be thrown fiercely in AIDS phantom!
    How soon, my friend, will hear Tom
    His girl-friend fervent magic moan?

---

34   Russian word 'bodiaga' corresponds an English word 'freshwater sponge', and has the same second meaning as the English one: nonsense, rot.English expression 'to talk through one's hat' sounds in Russian 'to sculpture a hunchback'.

35   In the verse make an accent in the word 'condom' on the second 'o'.

And is it possible for little John
To seize how rigid could it be condom.
Soon I've heard one knock and other,
My neighbor came for razzle-dazzle.
The girls have turned the player on,
Group revelry began to run!
If soon we have a deadly feast,
Let's play this French odd-even beast.
With huge headache when morning came
I set off see one busy man.
"Reveal the secret, clever Jake,
Do AIDS exist or it is fake.
I have no fear of HIV[36] disease
But what can I do with all my kids?
I can explain my little son
When leaving night-pot wipe your bum.
I am also able teach him how
A spirochaete[37] be turned down.
But destination of condom
Alas! I'd only say pardon!"
The clever man's respond was short:
"How can you be such idiot?
Can you imagine baby birth
Not having sexual intercourse?
Just tell to all who scared of HIV
Let drink instead 'Borzhom' or tea.
And sweat expansion to prevent
Let dress the coat in a bed.
And to protect from spittle spray

---

36   HIV – is the abbreviation for Human Immunodeficiency Virus.

37   Spirochaete – a genus of bacteria which causes syphilis; to turn down a spirochaete one must wash the genitals with regular soap right after the sexual intercourse.

A vow of silence should to say.
Then go along your own way
My time is precious waste for play."
I lost my doubts for all the times,
I understood: AIDS contrived.
All of this noisy AIDS mess
Falsification made from East to West.
But what the people have to say,
They maybe think another way?
And like the Russian poet great[38]
I went on streets for public straight.
 A passer-by said me at once
 "AIDS disease beats 'pederas'[39].
 Be friend of sports, leave off the glass,
 And virus will choose putans'[40] address."
I dropped in scientific place,
Met many scholars any race.
"A lot of critics blame AIDS,
But we need science, not a blitz.
AIDS and Cancer: close or not
Discern them really quite a lot.
But if you lose immune respond,
Keep looking trace in your hold.
Try to remember: soul and body
Tied very close in human logic ."
 I left this scientific place
 Advised be wise and be sustained.
 To have strong children nothing else
 Both Mom and Dad must have strong health.

---

38 **Nekrasov** in the poem *Who is happy in Russia?*

39 **Khrushchev** preferred to say 'pederas' instead of 'pederast'.

40 Putana – French word for a prostitute.

But if conceiving being drunk
AIDS and Cancer could be wrung.
And here came a merry man
With alcohol and garlic smell.
"Drink, dearly fellow, Russian quass[41]
That can destroy not only flies.
But maybe you are not so strong
And need catheter or a probe.
Well-known journal[42] chanted bells
Not knowing what is good for health.
Not try to clarify the truth
Campaign for currency began to use."
    And then I saw a lovely woman
    Standing alone in lights of neon[43].
    She had a fair Russian plait,
    Calm inner beauty, pensive face.
"Don't scare us, gentlemen, just cease,
We want to live, give birth to kids.
In spring bellowing furious bull
Much more attractive any rules[44].
We are not softies, are not whiners
We are great people in work and idling[45].
You need to know, you, brainless jerk,
Peaceful and mighty is Russian folk.

---

41   Quass – traditional Russian beverage produced from the bread (in English – malt).

42   Popular Russian magazine 'Ogoniok' ('Small light' in English) appealed to broad public to make donations needed to buy from abroad the disposable medical instruments (including catheters) to fight AIDS.

43   Inspired by the play of **Radzinskiy** *I stand by the restaurant: to marry is too late, to croak is to early. A monologue of a woman.*

44   This piece is inspired by the novel of **Ehrenburg** *Thirteen pipes.*

45   This is the paraphrase from the poem of **Nekrasov** *Who is Happy in Russia?*

He has no fear and so on
He is wise Titan, not condom."
    Along the streets, no wrong or right,
    Youth merry praising made all night.
    Kept romping, tricking, making fool,
    The life enjoying to the full.
August 6, 1989

In the USSR there was a very nice cartoon about tom-cat Leopold who was bothered by funny mice. At the end of every part Leopold kept saying to the mice: "Lads, let us live friendly!"

Finishing this chapter of the book I would like to repeat Leopold's appeal: "Two great countries, let us live friendly!"

UKRAINE

AMERICAN PROVERB: Good fences make good neighbors.

This book is mostly about the past. But talking about Ukraine one cannot forget the August 2008 events in Georgia and concealed threats of Russia toward the Ukraine's territory - the Crimea.

The author was born in the Ukraine, in its capital - Kiev City that was founded at the beginning of 6-th century A.C., circa 1500 years ago. Kiev City is much older than Moscow City, which was founded in 12-th century A.C. And the State of Kiev-Russia that later was transformed into Russia began its existence from approximately 882 A.C. (9th century).

So, it is ridiculous to hear now the opinion like those: "Ukraine cannot be an independent state from the geopolitical point of view???" "The Russia is the older brother of the Ukraine???"

Once upon a time the great Ukrainian man **Shevchenko** asked: "Why on the earth that full of milk and honey so much need and grief?"

Really: why?

This is a rhetorical question, and everybody can try to answer by oneself.

Ukrainian people are cordial, friendly, and hospitable. One Ukrainian woman said: "In every hut a hostess would pour the milk, propose the bread."

The Ukrainians are very sociable people. They will help in misfortune, will share a joy. They are strictly economical and at the same time simple-hearted and naive to some degree.

And Ukrainians have a strong sense of humor. The anecdotes in this chapter are mainly due to this feature.

<Beautiful Nataliya born in the Kiev City is attending an American real estate school. The American teacher asks her: "How are you? Do you understand me?"

Nataliya: "I do not know English, but I completely understand all you are talking about!">

<Ukrainian and a foreigner from a warm country are in the train compartment.

The foreigner put on the table the exotic fruits.

"What is it?" Ukrainian asks.

"This is a banana" the foreigner answers.

"Give me to taste."

"Treat yourself"- the foreigner offers.

"And what is it?" Ukrainian asks again looking at the other fruit.

"It is a mango."

"Give me to taste."

"Help yourself."

Then the Ukrainian takes a big piece of lard out of his bag and begins to eat with a great pleasure cutting the lard by small slices with a small knife.

"What is it?" the foreigner asks.

"It is a lard" the Ukrainian answers.

"Give me to taste" the foreigner asks.

"Why do you need to taste? A lard as a lard," Ukrainian answers.

<The court proceeding.

One man is charging for the rape.

An interrogation of a witness by a Judge is in action.

The Judge: "Describe, please, what you saw on the crime scene."

The witness: "I am going down and seeing: this man is shagging this woman."

The Judge: "Sir, you are in the court. Watch your language, please."

The witness: "And how I need to say?"

The prosecutor is prompting: "You should say a "sexual intercourse."

The witness continues:

"So what, I am going by and seeing a sexual intercourse. Then I am coming closer, and, oh, Lord, this man is shagging this woman.">

<A train is crossing the border between Ukraine and Russia.

A customs official is coming to the compartment and asks the Ukrainian man: "What do you carry with yourself? Do you have weapon? Do you have drugs?"

"Sure," the man answers.

"Show me," the customs official demands.

The Ukrainian is showing a piece of meat.

"But this is a lard," the customs official is laughing.

"But it's really a dope," the Ukrainian says. "When you begin to eat, you are not able to stop.">

Many Ukrainians are very courageous like their two greatest representatives Taras **Shevchenko** and Lesya **Ukrainka**. They both were the outstanding poets. They both fought for the Ukrainian national idea. They both suffered a lot. And they both had never surrendered.

Here is the verse of Lesya **Ukrainka**. She has written this verse when she was 19 years old, severely sick.

CONTRA SPEM SPERO! (Hope without Hope)

Get away, gloomy thoughts, autumn clouds!
Now, look, golden spring outside!
Is it true that in sorrow, in weeping
Youthful times would elapse, passing by.
    No, I want smiling through tears,
    Seeing trouble, to sing merry songs,
    With no hope keeping hope year by year,
    I want live! Get away gloomy thoughts!
Into virgin sorrowful soil
I shall plant lovely flowers omen,
I keep sowing the flowers when freezing,
I shall pour bitter tears on them.
    These hot tears will cause melting down
    Icy crust which is solid and flint,
    May be flowers would rise, then will coming
    For me also newborn jolly spring.
Up steep mountain rising in heaven
Big hard stone I'll be lifting alone,
This huge weight carrying calmly and even,
I'll be singing the bright merry song.
    During long murky night in a calmness
    I shan't close any moment my eyes:

Searching dear guiding star in the darkness,
Beaming sovereign of mysterious nights.
Yes! I'll keep smiling through tears,
Seeing trouble shall sing merry songs,
With no hope do keep hope year by year,
I shall live! Get away gloomy thoughts!

There is one place in the Ukraine that attracts close attention of many people. This is the Odessa City on the Black Sea shore.

Odessa is the warm bright city with lovely women and witty men. It has a nickname "A pearl by the sea."

Here are two cute anecdotes full of Odessa's charm.

<Newly arrived man stops a stout Odessa-man who is bringing a big water-melon pressing it by hands to his stomach.

Newly arrived man asks: "Help me, please, to find the Bank-street."

"Take a water-melon for a second," Odessa-man asks.

Newly arrived man takes a water-melon.

Odessa-man makes a broad helpless gesture with his arms and produces the expression of ignorance on his face.

Then he takes the water-melon back and continues his way.>

<Newly arrived man stops Odessa-man and asks the way to the Deribassovskaya-street[46]?"

Odessa-man answers: "You need to go straight down this street, then turn left and take a tram which is going to the Privoz[47]. In the Privoz you need to buy a rooster. And then

---

46   Deribassovskaya-street is the main and very famous street in Odessa City.

47   Privoz is the famous market in Odessa City.

twist the balls to the rooster not to me. You are standing on the Deribassovskaya- street" (an expression 'to twist the balls' means 'to make a fool of somebody '). >

Ukraine is not a big country. But she[48] has a warm soul, is beautiful, many people call her "Nen'ka" (mother). She has Kiev City, Odessa City, many other renowned cities, and she has of course the Dnieper River glorified by great **Gogol**:

"Miraculous is the Dnieper in still weather when, quietly and fluently, he[49] is tearing down through the forests and the mountains his full waters. No rustle; no thunder. You are looking and unaware, is it going or not going his stately width, and it's seems as though the whole of him is molded out of a glass, and as if the blue unruffled way, excessively in width, endlessly in length, is flying and winding along the green world. It is a pleasure at that time both for hot sun to look round from its height and to dip its rays into the coldness of the glass waters and for riverside forests to be reflected brightly in the waters. Green-curly! they are crowding together with the wild flowers toward the waters, and bending over are looking into them, and never tired of looking, and never tired of admiring by their bright reflection, and are smiling to him[50], and are greeting him nodding their branches. But into the very middle of the Dnieper they do not dare to look: nobody, except of the sun and the blue sky, never look into him. A rare bird is able to fly to the middle of the Dnieper. Splendid! He has no equal river all over the world."

(**Gogol**. *The Terrible Vengeance* 1831).

---

48   Ukraine has a feminine gender.

49   Dnieper River has a masculine gender.

50   To the Dnieper River.

THE RUSSIANS AND THE FOREIGNERS

RUSSIAN EXPRESSION: What is good for Russian is a death for German.[51]

WILLIAM SAROYAN: The Slav is himself first and his race afterwards, while the Teuton is his race first and himself afterwards.

(*The Daring Young Man on the Flying Trapeze...*)

These two conceptions are very complicated and demand thorough analysis.

At this time I am not able to do this, have no intention to offend anybody. I only wish to propose to the reader to give rise for free associations when actualizing in the consciousness these two maxims.

The Russians treat the foreigners usually kindly, with soft humor and concealed interest. Here are two anecdotes.

<Russian man is fishing in the Thames River.
A policeman is going by and says:
"Sir, it is prohibited to fish in this place."
The policeman is going away.
After half an hour the policeman is coming back.

---

51   **Gogol**: "We call everybody 'German' who is just from the foreign lands." 'German' sounds in Russian 'nemetz' which is close to Russian word 'nemoy' (mute). So: the one who cannot speak Russian language is the mute for Russian people.

The Russian man answers:

"I am not fishing. I am just bathing my favorite worm.">

<A fire began in the prostitute house in Paris.

Shouts: "Fire! Fire! Bring water!"

A voice of the Russian customer: "And two mugs of beer!">

The Russian will always return a slight remark, his word have to be final.

<Russian man works as a sewage-disposal person in the Warsaw.

In the morning a Polish woman opens a window in her apartment and asks: "What is the time, Mr. Sh-t -collector?"

"It is 4 a.m. now, Missis Bi-ch.">

The Russians' endurance to vodka is fabulous. Here is an excellent anecdote.

<A foreigner writes a letter to his homeland.

"Yesterday I drank vodka with the Russians. I was nearly to die. Today we drank samogon.[52] Better if I died yesterday!">

Sometimes the Russians are unable to understand the foreigners.

<A Russian-man is strolling down the London's street.

Before him an English-man is walking having bananas in his ears.

---

52 Samogon is Russian rough home-distilled vodka.

"Sir, bananas are in your ears," Russian is shouting.
English-man stops and is taking bananas off the ears:
"Sir, speak louder, there are bananas in my ears.">

<Russian student offended China student.
China student said: "I shall revenge myself."
The Russian student just smiled.
In the middle of the night the Russian student woke up because of a heavy dream. He saw a big stone on his stomach with the inscription: "Chinese revenge."
Russian student laughed and threw the stone out of the window from the seventh floor.
During the seconds his testicles were torn off.">

I suppose that relations between the Russians and
the foreigners are an eternal enigma. From the one side, we know some Russia foreign rulers who are like saints for the Russian people. From the other side, some Russians tear away foreigners, especially from the former republics of the USSR.

Really, the Lord paths are inscrutable!

SOCCER

RUSSIAN SONG: Hey, goalkeeper, meet the combat,
You are a sentry at the goals.[53]
Be aware: the country boundary
Lined exactly your back beyond.

(The song is from the popular movie of 30-th *Goalkeeper)*

Soccer is the sport number one in many countries.

In the former USSR the high authorities called soccer as the "Communist Party's sport" due to the great meaning of achievements in soccer for the country prestige.

The elite soccer players all times had hotly devoted love of the population and all conceivable privileges. Many years the soccer team number one in the former Soviet Union was the great team "Dynamo Kiev" from Ukraine.

Living in Kiev the author of this book had many occasions to meet and sometimes to interact with great athletes. So, I would like to share some reminiscences about the greats.

Valeriy Vasil'evich **Lobanovskiy** was outstanding soccer player and coach. We have met in 1954 in the youth soccer team (up to 18 years old). One forward of the team was disqualified for five games, and the team coach has substituted

---

53   Goalkeeper – a player in the soccer game who must defend the goals from scoring by the opponent. Goals – two upright posts joined at the top by a horizontal crossbar. A goal is scored when the whole of the ball passes over the goal line between the goalposts and under the crossbar.

him by the talented player from the children team (up to 16 years old). This was **Lobanovskiy**.

He was pretty closed for interactions. I dare to say he was shy enough. This time I even did not know his first name, maybe because of a big distance between us on the soccer field - he was a left wing forward (left winger)[54], I was a goalkeeper. Anyway, everybody could clearly see the enormous soccer aptitudes of the young player.

We have happened upon in several years. This time I did not succeed to become the professional soccer player, and **Lobanovskiy** was invited to the "Dynamo Kiev", the highest rank soccer team. During this second meeting he told me about his failure to be the player of "Dynamo" Kiev team, about his intention to give up the high rank soccer, and to pay close attention for his study in the Kiev Polytechnic institute to have a profession of an engineer.

After three months we have met by chance again. This time **Lobanovskiy** played constantly as the left winger in the "Dynamo" Kiev team and was invited to the USSR national soccer team.

Now his monument is erected at one of the famous Kiev City stadium which bears his name.

The next reminiscence is intended to illustrate people's love to the soccer stars.

I had a dinner in one of the Kiev City restaurant - small, popular, comfy. It was daytime, only two tables were

---

54 At those times the main tactical system was 1+3+2+5: goalkeeper + three full backs, or defenders (center, right and left) + two halfbacks (right and left) + five forwards, or attackers (right and left wingers, right and left insights and center forward).

Halfback (now - midfielder) – performs the functions of defense and participates in attacking actions of a team. From the area of joke: in the former USSR policeman was called 'halfback'.

occupied. Close to me a couple of very decent middle-aged women dined.

All of a sudden a noisy group of young males came in the restaurant and settled beside of our tables. Two very famous soccer players were in the group.

One of them was already well gone, silent and almost slept all the time. The other - was moderately intoxicated, in the stage of talkativeness, and used the obscene words any couple of seconds. It is necessary to remind that the Russian curses are much stronger and various than in any other language.

The women were shocked, I was perplexed. I had to do something to calm the cursing one; on the other side, I was a little bit acquainted with both stars, and did not want to attract their close attention.

Then out of a blue I have found the right decision. I informed the women that they are sitting very close to the soccer celebrities, and revealed the names of them. Next moment the women did not hear anything trying to make close examination of the stars.

"Is it really player X?" one woman asked looking at the talkative one. "I am going to remember these celebrities and to tell about my meeting with them to all my relatives and friends."

Now I would like to present some of the soccer folklore by the lips of the soccer coaches.

Different soccer coaches use different verbal means to tune the players and whole team for a victory. Here are the examples of soccer coaches' parting words instantly before the team leaves a locker room for the game.

\<Don't say 'If'. If a grandmother has testicles she would be a grandfather.\>

<You can get either a chest full of orders or a head in the bushes.>

It is also very interesting to watch for some coaches and to listen at their instant reproofs during the game.

<"Jap (for 'Japanese'), one more time you undertake a pettiness[55] in our penalty area, and I would tear your testicles off! ">

<"El (for 'Elephant'), where is your right foot?" This retort was made after the player scored a goal by a header[56].>

<"Ben, what are you doing? You are making a sliding-tackle[57] like a pregnant woman.">

Soccer game is the perfect model for studying human relations.

There is a popular Russian song "When we were young!" (Lyrics of the song were written by Yunna **Moritz**). In the song one can find the lovely lines:

"When we were young,
And talking finest nonsense,
Blue fountains have been spurted out,
Red roses have been blossomed up!"

---

55 Pettiness – very short passes of the ball in the restricted area. Penalty area – this is the area which is very close to the goals.

56 Header – this is a strike to the ball by the head.

57 Sliding tackle – this is a soccer technique which is a last-ditch effort to kick the ball away from an opponent's feet or to gain ball possession by means of sideway body slide over the ground when an opponent is going to get past.

When our parents were young the soccer game was romantic. Those times the accent was placed on the attack, there were no super defensive constructions. And main thing: teams wanted to have only a fair victory. It lasted approximately till the 50th of the last century.

When we were young, beginning from 60th, the soccer game began to change its priorities. Much more attention was paid on defense, a number of defenders were increased, were introduced the very strict demands for the discipline during the game. The bets have been significantly raised.

Year after year the price of the victory was constantly growing, and the idea of using the supplemental means for achieving the victory was born little by little.

One famous specialist of soccer game enunciated the following maxim: "The main thing in the sports and especially in the soccer game is a victory. How to reach the one! First of all your team must be strong in all components: talented players, adequate physical, technical, tactical preparation. Then psychological readiness: moral preparation, high motivation. And. Imagine that your team is going to meet the team that has the same qualities. What you should do to win? It is not a rhetorical question. Yes, you are right: to find the additional means!"

The first additional means was a referee of the game, the second - a dope.

I remember the talking in the soccer circles about the gifts for a referee of an international game. Someone told me that high soccer authorities discussed this question and un-official ruled what price of the object consist a gift and what price - a bribe. I propose for the reader to decide: is mink fur coat for the referee's wife the gift or the bribe?

Using a dope for the soccer players is a very difficult scientific problem. What kind of a dope? Is it necessary to apply the dope for all members of the team or for some players? What the physiological and psychological player's resistance for the dope? What is the best time to apply the dope? How often is possible to use a dope?

However, if the dope is applied "adequately", the team gets the very serious advantages against the approximately equal opposite team.

I remember one game during the World Soccer Championship of 1982 in Spain between two international teams of a very high class. One team from the very beginning proposed so high tempo, so rigid one-to-one combats that the performance of the opposite team reminded the one in a rapid movie shooting. The final result of the game was done in the first half of the first 45-minutes of the game.

But you can ask: if the second team would use the same means?

So, the next step is to bribe the coach or some players from the opposite team. It is not necessary to do much. During the equal play one intentional mistake of goalkeeper or stopper[58], or intentional wrong action of the coach can decide the fate of the game.

Anything does not stay unchanged in our dialectical world. The strong contemporarily organizations could find the more essential means. For example, alternations: to-day you are a Champion, a Winner, a Triumphant, to-morrow - me, the day after tomorrow - that bloke[59].

---

58 Stopper – this is a player from defenders who must crush opponent's attacks in the central zone (most dangerous for scoring). Usually this player is tall, strongly built, very aggressive, rigid and skillful in one-to-one marking.

59 That bloke – the specific expression from the Russian folklore when somebody wants to hint that we are obliged to do something for the one who doesn't exist now.

The only one thing is left to hit upon in this chapter: the moral estimation of the dishonest deeds.

Once upon a time when the USSR still existed there were the soccer all-Union championships. Every year the championship lasted about nine months, and was the greatest public event. There was a tradition together with the main prizes to award a prize for the best goal-scorer of the championship.

During one championship two goal-scorers from two teams were leading for the prize being very close in the amount of the scored goals. Before the last game of the season these two teams with the players-contestants were not in the equivalent positions. The last game of the first team was very important for both teams that participated in this game. The last game of the second team could not decide anything for both participating in the game teams. The prize was won by the player-contestant from the second team, who scored in the game five goals.

The scorer-winner received good financial reward from the team management. But I am trying to understand the chain of thoughts of the winner. Did he really have the moral satisfaction?

Before 1990 soviet soccer super-stars could not play in the international super-clubs. In 1986 I watched the final game of the World soccer championship with one of such a star. He was a coach then, but commented the actions of the players as if he was their colleague in the field. His eyes and voice were very sad. He did not yet know that in a couple of years the door abroad for the players of his rank will be open.

ARMENIAN RADIO

The book is going to the end. It would be a big mistake not to mention one more group of the anecdotes produced by people as an "Armenian radio."

There is a very beauty country on the Caucasian mountains - Armenia state; the former Armenian Soviet Socialistic Republic in the former USSR.

The country is inhabited by very clever, very witty and very kind people - Armenians. Nobody knows if all "Armenian Radio" anecdotes were produced by the Armenians. Anyway the anecdotes are very witty and very nice.

Of course, the group has the cute anecdotes about sex.

<The Armenian radio is asked: "Can woman be pregnant from the valerian drops."

The Armenian radio answers: "Yes, she can, if Valerian is at least 14 year old boy.">

<The Armenian radio is asked: "Why a cow has so sad eyes?"

The Armenian radio answers: "Imagine if a woman be pulled by the breasts every day and slept with a man once a year, what kind of eye expression she would have.">

There also non-sexual but all the same very witty anecdotes.

<The Armenian radio is asked: "Is it possible to be killed by an electric current if you would stand by foot on the train rail?"

The Armenian radio answers: "Yes, you can be killed if you would manage to cast your second foot on the power supply wire.">

<The Armenian radio is asked: "What the longest Russian last name is known?"

The Armenian radio answers: "And joined them **Shepilov**[60]".>

<The Armenian radio is asked: "What is it: all around the water and in the middle is a fear?"

The Armenian radio answers: "An attorney procurator is taking a bath."

And what is it: "All around is a fear and in the middle is the water?"

Answer: "An attorney procurator is drinking tea.">

And I would like to present at the end of the chapter my favorite anecdote.

<The Armenian radio is asked: "What is necessary to do to prevent a fur falling out of a throat-wrap?

Answer: "We do not know what it is a throat-wrap (in Russian "gorzhetka") but can make a guess: it is necessary not to bicycle frequently.">

---

60 The soviet media in 1957: "The anti-party group consisting the former big party bosses **Malenkov, Molotov, Kaganovich** and joined them **Shepilov** was expelled from the rows of the CPSU.

CONCLUSION

The Russia has a very complex and difficult history. In 19th century one of the best times account of it – *The History of the State of Russia* - was written by outstanding Russian historian Nikolay Mikhailovich **Karamzin**.

Another famous Russian man, count Alexey Konstantinovich **Tolstoy** wrote the poem regarding Russian history from the very beginning[61] till the first half of 19th century. Here is the poem in an abridged translation.

THE HISTORY OF THE STATE OF RUSSIA
So, listen, lads, the story
Old man to tell you need.
That our land is wealthy,
Just order does not keep.

This very truth, my dearest,
Millennium ago
Grasped our forefathers:
No order, just ado.

---

61   Karamzin is beginning the history of Russia state from 862 A.C., when Slavs being tired of inner discords called three brothers Varangians (Rurik, Sineus, Truvor) who became the first rulers in the ancient Russia and due to whom she received her name.

They gathered under banner
And talking: "What to do?
Let's go to Varangians:
And ask them come to rule."

The messengers so promptly
Went to the needed place
Are saying to Varangians:
"Come, gentlemen! Don't waste!"

And then three brothers coming,
Varangians of middle age,
They see: the land is wealthy,
Just order does not have.

The older brother **Rurik**[62]
Was Prince for many years,
The land was still abundant
But order did not have!
Then ruler was Prince Igor,
But actually Oleg[63],
Who was great ruthless warrior
And clever man, not brag.

---

62 **Rurik** ruled seventeen years in the Novgorod City – one of the most ancient city of the Eastern Slavs first mentioned in 859 A.C.

63 Prince **Rurik** when dying handed the ruling of the state and guardianship for his young son Igor to his relative Oleg. Approximately in 882 A.C. Prince Oleg treacherously killed Kiev's princes Askold and Dir, seized Kiev City, and included it in the Russian state. He also uttered the prophetic words: "This will be the mother of all cities of Rus (short word for Russia)." Actually from this time the history of Russia state is beginning; some historians prefer to name the State in this period as Kievan Rus (Kiev City Russia).

Then was the Princess Olga[64]
Her after – Svyatoslav.[65]
Such was a strict succession
The rulers of pagan Slavs.

And when the Prince Vladimir
Acceded father's throne,
The end of old religion
Soon came to Russian home.[66]

He suddenly told people:
"Sure, our Gods are trash,
Let's christening in water
Have monotheism by slash!"

"Perun[67] is too repulsive!
When pushing him away,
The nice and goodly order
We'll set up for long way!"

For priests he sent the missions
To Athens and Tsargrad,[68]
A lot of priests came promptly,
Make crosses, incense burn.

---

64   Princess Olga, the spouse of Prince Igor, ruled after his death.

65   Prince Svyatoslav was the son of Prince Igor and Princess Olga, the first Russian
     Prince who had Slavonic name.

66   After the death of Prince Svyatoslav in 972 A.C. his three sons began to quarrel
     with each other. Yaropolk who ruled in Kiev City killed Oleg, then Vladimir
     killed Yaropolk an d ruled Russia from 980 through 1015 A.C. Prince Vladimir
     converted Russia into Christianity in 988 A.C.

67   Perun was the main pagan God of Slavs, the deity of thunder and lightning.

68   Tsargrad –'the city of the Tsar' in Russian, the ancient Constantinople, those
     times the capital of Byzantium Empire.

Sing nicely and touching
And filling their bags;
The land, as such, abundant,
But order does not have.

Vladimir died due sorrow,[69]
No order setting now.
And soon began the ruling
His son prince Yaroslav.

Under the rule of this one
The order could be done,
But having love to children
All land he shared for sons.

It was not good decision,
And children after all,
Began to punch each other:
When fighting for the throne.

The Tatars got to know
These things and thinking "Vus"!
Wide trousers are putting,
Rushed promptly on the Rus.

"Look! Your controversy
The earth turned upside-down,
Wait just for our version,
And order will be done".

---

69   Vladimir's son Yaroslav tried to make a military conflict with his father.

They yelled: "Keep giving tribute!"
(No way to save the face.)
And here all sorts of rubbish
Tormented our space.

Each new day brother on brother
Brings slander to the Horde[70];
Yes, our land was wealthy –
But order did not have.

Then Ivan Third[71] came ruling
And said: "No more dig!
From our knees we're rising!"
And sent to Tatars fig.

And now no harm and evil
There was in our Land.
Fertile in bread and butter,
Bur order did not have.

The Ivan Fourth[72] then coming,
Grandson of Ivan Third.
Firm as a rock in ruling
And many wives was spouse.

---

70   Russia was conquered by Tatar hordes which were ruled by Tatar khans.
Here the word 'Horde' means the Tatar representative in Russia who used to
take the tribute and the slander.

71   Ivan Third was a sovereign, Grand Duke – ruled 1462-1505; he had thrown
down the Tatar khans yoke.

72   Ivan Fourth – Tsar Ivan the Fourth "Terrible", ruled 1533-1584; in 1582 he
killed his oldest son Ivan, the heir of the Russian throne.

He was first Tsar of Russia,
And "Terrible" nicknamed.
Because being like fastness
All solid, always grave.

He was not sweet companion,
Had mind far from thin,
He introduced the order -
Land empty, not a thing.

Then after him was Fyodor[73],
Quite contrast to his dad.
Had mind not so broad,
Talk rubbish only good.

Tsar's relative, the Boris[74]
Was clever, often con.
Dark-haired, rather handsome
Has sat on regal throne.

His reign was pretty smoothly,
Old evils have been ceased.
He was too close to settle
The order on the Rus.

Unfortunately Impostor[75]
Came out of the blue,
Made fuss and real disaster
So, Boris-Tsar passed through.

---

73   Tsar Fyodor Ivanovich, the son of Ivan the Fourth, ruled 1584-1598.

74   Tsar Boris **Godunov**, the brother-in-law of Tsar Fyodor, ruled 1598-1605.

75   'Impostor' – see in the *Vocabulary*.

He reached the throne and treasure
This insolent smart boy.
And with his bride sitting together
Legs dangling full of joy.

Although of being dashing,
And even far of fool,
His ruling was not special,
And even Poles broke rules.

We do not like such barrage,
And here in one night
We stroke them into terror,
And drove away in flight.

Ascended then Vasiliy[76],
But soon the one and all
Asked him "Do not be silly,
And leave away the throne."

The Poles came back with Cossacks
Full mess and scuffles done.
And then the anti-order
In our Land began.

There were a lot of passions -
Not spark of order yet.
It's well known if no power,
One cannot target hit.

---

76   Tsar Vasiliy Ivanovich **Shuyskiy**, ruled in 1606-1610.

Tsar's ruling to restore
And to support the truth
The people called heroes[77]
To stand for holy Rus.
This mighty force threw Poles
Again off, and so on,
We asked then young **Romanov**[78]
Ascend on Russian throne.

And many foreign countries
Sent due respect for us.
The land was too abundant
No order, only fuss.

Then Alexey **Romanov**[79]
Succeeded father's throne.
Then son of his named Pyotr[80]
Built Russia's real dome.

Tsar Peter loved the order
Almost like Tsar Ivan.
The same thing in relations,
Sometimes he has been drunk.

---

77   A citizen of Nizhniy Novgorod (the city on the Volga River) Kozma **Minin** and the prince Dmitriy **Pozharskiy** in 1612 gathered the people's volunteer corps and defeated the enemies.

78   The first Tsar of Romanovs' dynasty was Mikhail Fyodorovich **Romanov** who ruled Russia in 1613-1645 (he began his ruling being 16 years old).

79   Tsar Alexey Mikhaylovich **Romanov**, ruled in 1645-1676.

80   Peter I the Great (Pyotr) – ruled the Russian empire in 1682-1725; in 1718 his eldest son and heir Alexey was tortured and killed on father's order.

He said: "Without me, I pity,
You'll perish, nothing else;
My stick is good for people
Whom Father I declared.

No longer than on Christmas
You'll hear the order trump!"
And searching for the order
He left for Amsterdam.

When being back from there,
He smoothly shaved us, then
On Christmas, what a deal,
As Dutchmen dressed all Land.

This thing I say just joking,
I do not blame great Pyotr:
Prescribe a purge, I talking
For stomach not a fault.

Although these actions maybe
Are pretty strong and cruel;
However enough plenty
Was order when he ruled.

But suddenly he died,
Not being still too old,
And look, the Land of mine
No order has at all.

There were a lot of monarchs
In Russia after him.
Some - mild, some - too honored,
And many were Tsarin.[81]

The jolly lively Empress
There was Elizabeth:[82]
Just singing, merry-making,
But order did not have.

And what the cause of trouble,
And where is evil root,
That even great Tsarina[83]
Had failed reach the truth.

"Madam, with your ruling
The order will be made" -
Humanitarians[84] were cooing
So courteously and brave.

"Give your people freedom,
Whom Mother you're proclaimed,
Just freedom, give them freedom,
As quickly as you can."

---

81   Tsarina – the Empress of Russia.

82   Elizabeth – the Empress of Russia in 1741-1762, the daughter of Peter the
     Great and his second wife Catherine I, the Empress of Russia in 1725-1727.

83   Catherine II the Great, the Empress of Russia in 1762-1796; she took power
     after the conspiracy on July 1762 in result of which her husband Tsar Peter III
     (ruled six months in 1762) was killed.

84   French writer **Voltaire** (1694-1778) and French philosopher Denis **Diderot**
     (1713-1784).

"Messieurs," returned she nicely,
"You are so kind and all".
And instantly has fastened
Ukrainians to soil.[85]

Her minion dearest grandson[86]
Began his ruling then,
His nerves were not so icy,
But he was gentleman.

When in the big excitement
Napoleon moved to hit[87]
And so close was disaster,
He set up to retreat.

It seems, what could be worse
Be seated in such hole,
But look: our troops in Paris
God bless **Romanov**'s home.

This time really excessive
Bloomed Russia's world pride,
Our land still pretty wealthy,
But order not so fine.

---

85   Catherine the Great turned Ukrainians into the serfs.

86   Alexander I the Blessed, was the Emperor of Russia in 1801-1825. He succeeded
     to the throne after the conspiracy in which his father Paul I, the Emperor of
     Russia in 1796-1801, was murdered; historians do not have common opinion
     if Alexander participated in the conspiracy.

87   Invasion in Russia of the troops of Napoleon **Bonaparte** in 1812.

Compiled was from the true facts
This story short and brave,
By thin and humble novice
God's slave named Alexey[88].

Here is the end of the verse of the count **Tolstoy** and the narration of the historian **Karamzin**. Let's finish the short history of the great Russia.

I would like to begin with expressing my opinion regarding the Emperor Alexander I the Blessed. As the maxim from the Bible says: "There is no prophet in his own land!"

Being raised in the former USSR I can firmly say that both the Russian officials and soviet historians consciously or unconsciously or having special orders badly underestimate the grandeur of this historical person.

Under his wise ruling the Napoleon **Bonaparte** whose huge military forces terrified all Europe and the whole world were defeated. Initially Alexander I was caught between Scylla[89] - the necessity to withstand the growing threat of Napoleon - and Charybdis - to withstand this threat when many European countries and inner critics hampered and impeded him. He was patient, wise till the crucial point, and I think he defeated the Napoleon **Bonaparte** with the smallest possible losses.

Much later after him the 43rd President of the United States George Walker **Bush** was caught in the same Scylla-Charybdis situation, and in spite of huge amount of inner critics he cardinally settled the problem, came off with flying

---

88   Alexey Konstantinovich **Tolstoy.**

89   Scylla and Charybdis, to be between – two monsters in Greek mythology that lived on either side of a narrow sea strait; so the sailors attempting to avoid Scylla would pass too close to Charybdis, and vice versa.

colors. He did not believe in the negotiations with enemy, the same as his great predecessor.

The prominent Russian citizen **Krylov** wrote the famous fable due to the Napoleon's invasion and Russian victory. Here is the abridged translation of the fable.

THE WOLF IN THE KENNELS

One night the Wolf intending get into the sheep-fold,
Found himself into the kennels.
> And instantly was raised a general alarm.
> "Bring fire!" shouts sound, "bring fire!"
> The fire was brought.

The Wolf is sitting drove into the corner,
His teeth are chattering, his hair is bristling up,
Devouring everybody with his eyes sharp.
> However catching truth he ran across big power now
> And there's coming very moment
> For all killed animals to pay,
> Then, entered cunning one
> Into the parley.

And he began: "My friends!
Why did you make this noisy mess?
I am Godfather yours, any less,
And came to make it up with you,
Not in the least for quarrel;
And can affirm by my wolf's oath vow,
That me..."
> "You better listen me,"
> The huntsman cut him short.
> "You are the grey, but I am, buddy, have turned grey,

And nature of the wolves I know far ago.
So, therefore my custom is:

With wolves no other peaceful deeds,
Just take off their skins."
And instantly gave way for barking hounds.

Alexander I the Blessed was handsome, highly educated and wise. This Emperor who ruled in the beginning of 19th century introduced the freedom for publishing houses, prohibited the tortures. I cannot refuse to do the pleasure for myself citing the opinions about him. **Karamzin**: "We read in the fine soul of Alexander I a strong desire to confirm in Russia the priority of law. It's hardly to believe that anybody from the sovereigns excelled him in love, in zeal for the common weal, was so little dazzled by the luster of crown, and was so able to be a person on the throne as he was!" (p. 1004). And it's hardly to find anybody from the contemporary rulers who could be matched to this picture, with the exception maybe of Ronald **Reagan**, Margaret **Thatcher,** Golda **Meir**, Otto von **Bismarck**. Once great **Bismarck** said: "Vanity is a mortgage that must be deducted from the value of a man" (see: book of Erich **Eyck**). Did you identify any contemporary ruler with big vanity?

Here is excerpt from the book of Alan **Palmer**.

President Thomas **Jefferson** six years after Alexander's accession on the throne: "A more virtuous man, I believe, does not exist, nor one who is enthusiastically devoted to better the condition of mankind."

British Foreign Secretary **Castlereagh:** I knew "of no Sovereign in history who has had so rich a harvest of glory".

Then was the reign of Alexander's I younger brother, the Emperor of Russia Nikolay I, from 1825 through 1855. He was rigid, many persons supposed him to be cruel, with strong will, strong ruling. He was a guardian against revolutions in Europe. Especially he is smeared by official soviet history.

After him came on the Russian throne his eldest son. It was Alexander II, Tsar Liberator, the Emperor of Russia in 1855-1881. He was very progressive ruler, implemented many challenging reforms, especially the emancipation of the serfs in 1861. In spite of his liberal course, human dignity he was constantly a target for assassinations (1866, 1873, 1880) by quickly arousing Russian terrorist movement. At last he was killed in public by terrorists in 1881 during well-prepared conspiracy.

He was succeeded by his son Alexander III, who was the Emperor of Russia in 1881-1894. Alexander III was noted of his immense physical strength, was rigid and, the most important, was an anti-Semite. His anti-Semitic policy (such as the restrictions for Jews the area of a settlement, the occupations which Jew does not have a right to attain) encouraged the Jewish emigration to the United States from 1880 on. I think this barbaric policy continued by his successor Tsar Nikolay II, contributed so much to the Bolsheviks upheaval in 1917.

Then came the time of the last Russian Emperor, Nikolay II, "Bloody Nikolay", son of Alexander III. He ruled 1894-1917. Everybody knows, I suppose, that in 1917 Nikolay II abdicated the throne, then Bolsheviks upheaval happened, and then, in the July of 1918, the Bolsheviks have shot in the basement room all the family of the last Russian Tsar: him, his wife, five children and the personal of four persons, including the personal physician of the family, the son of the famous Russian clinician **Botkin.** I would like to name his children killed by Bolsheviks: Olga (23 years old), Tatyana (21), Maria (19), Anastasia (17), and the heir of the throne

Tsarevich Alexey (14). Nikolay II was the one who could be characterized by the famous Russian saying "How little roads have been walked how many errors have been done."

Then "The Cursed Days" came.

This name great **Bunin** gave to his book in which he described the days right after the Bolsheviks upheaval and expressed his aversion to the Bolsheviks' regime characterizing the Soviet government as "a disgusting gallery of convicts."

I am not going to describe all horrors of Bolsheviks' crimes during and after upheaval of 1917, during the Civil war in Russia. I prefer to give the word to the famous Russian woman **Gippius** who was a spectator of the events. Her verses about 1917 upheaval:

To please what devil and what a dog, indeed,
The people in nightmarish dreams,
Had killed insanely their own freedom,
And even did not kill - just whipped to death?

We are lying smeared and tied,
All the corners through,
Sailors'[90] spittle have been spread
Our foreheads like a glue.

In her book **Gippius** describing the first years after Bolsheviks upheaval, condemns England, France, Finland and Sweden in actual support the Bolsheviks. She writes: "The England straight away 'began to speak' to Bolsheviks. The France was led by England; that is why so absurd her verbal

---

90   Sailors – in Russian 'matrosy', the lowest navy rank, actively supported the
      Bolsheviks' 1917 upheaval.

'recognitions of **Wrangel**'[91] with simultaneous sending the delegations to the Bolsheviks. Only Poland fought against the Bolsheviks" (pp. 395, 403).

Then the Russia met concentration camps, millions of innocent victims.

After that, in 1932-33, the disastrous starvation came to the Ukraine and caused the death about 10 millions of the Ukrainian peasants. The starvation was named as 'Holodomor' from Ukrainian words 'holod' (hunger) and 'mor' (plague) - so the death from hunger or murder by hunger.

This time the Ukraine was a part of the USSR and the main producer of the grain in the international scale. Now it is very important, I suppose, to determine the real reason of 'Holodomor'.

The roots of 'Holodomor' are the subject of the scholarly debate. The scholars have two opposite points of view: 1) this was a consequence of the economic changes implemented during the period of the Soviet industrialization, and 2) the Soviet authorities designed the famine intentionally attacking the rise of Ukrainian nationalism, so it was the genocide. Let us try to make our own decision.

At the end of 20th-beginning of 30th the communists from Moscow and Saint Petersburg came to the Ukraine and began to seize from Ukrainian peasants their individual farms; more reach families were turned out of their homes, arrested and deported to Siberia.[92]

Then much more communists came from the Russia to the Ukraine and began to seize grain, food, even dishes which were cooking in the ovens. And the sacramental question

---

91   Baron **Wrangel** – see the *Name Directory*.

92   Siberia is the vast region in the Asian part of Russia with severe climate, short summer, the place of exile and concentration camps.

is rising: why they needed such a huge amount of grain instantly?

Not to feed the builders of industrialization because many of them were the prisoners or were going to be the prisoners of communists' concentration camps? Even to mention this thing is ridiculous.

To remove the danger of the nationalism that was growing? It is ridiculous again. The communists used to remove any danger for themselves just killing their opponents.

But I am going to agree with the modern Ukrainian dictionary that describes 'Holodomor' as 'artificial hunger, organized in a vast scale by the criminal regime against the country's population. My suggestion: it was necessary to throw a vast amount of grain on the international market targeting to cut substantially the prices and to kill finally the American farmers who suffered from overproduction during the Great Depression.

Then the Great Depression of 1929-1939. Why so serious, so crushing?

I can only make some suggestions from the psychological point of view.

Stock market crashed in October 29, 1929. This time the speculative urge had seized many people who, as **Watkins** says in his book *The Great Depression*, swallowed the golden bait; many amateur stock buyers have been manipulated like in a shell game (p.33).

The first question: could be the manipulations and the crash intentionally done by some strong world power. My answer is 'Yes', at least in a very big part.

Watkins also says that due to the general agreement the crash of stock market itself did not "cause" the Great Depression. "We still do not know," he says, "with any overwhelming certainty why it was that the biggest and most productive economy on the planet inexorably disintegrated during the three years after the closing gong sounded on the floor of the New York Stock Exchange on October 29, 1929 (p.41)."

Then **Watkins** names main reasons between which are the most important overproduction and banking system failing.

Overproduction was partly due to the monopoly (by 1929 some two hundred corporations controlled almost half of all American industry), partly by intentional cut (suggested above) the international agricultural market prices by Russian communists.

The causes of banking system failure were the same as now, in 2008-09 in the so-called crisis. **Watkins** cites the Louisiana banking commissioner who in 1925 has analyzed the bank failures in his state: "Gross and evil management, poor management, promotion of speculative enterprises, loans without security, too large loans, loans to companies in which officers were interested, were the major causes of bank failure" (p.47). Failing banks took with them millions of dollars in deposits which were at that time uninsured.

It is not necessary to reason a lot to understand that this "bank operation" was intentionally planned with the aim to rob depositors and to crash the financial stability of the country by the enemies of the United States both inner and international.

The unemployment was the disastrous result of the above mentioned factors.

Watkins in his book on the page 82 pronounces, I think, the key words that explain the Great Depression - **"Organizing Wrath."** Many people and organizations all over the world hated and hate now the Great America which stirs the envy up, irritates by its prominent achievements, including the achievement in the areas of human rights' defense and people's welfare. Some envious creatures are trying to dirty the country and its values, some - are harboring a big grudge trying to destroy USA. Who were the enemies? Mostly Russian and American communists were.

Communist-sponsored "hunger marches" all over the country, a lot of incidents of violence and subversion, strikes, marches in many cities, intermittent agricultural strikes, migrant farm workers' agricultural strikes, battles on the ground of Ford Motor company, many eruptions of public unrest between the winter of 1930 and the winter of 1933 luridly chronicled in the daily press.

In 1933 President Franklin Delano **Roosevelt** formally recognized the USSR, and the diplomatic relations has been reestablished.

Watkins: "The conservative doomsayers were certainly right about one thing: the Communist Party/USA was helping to nurture rebellion industriously where and when it could" (p.82).

Nearly six months before the stock market crush the soviet leader **Stalin** ventured a prediction to a small group of American Communists: "I think that the moment is not far off when a revolutionary crisis will develop in America (**Watkins**, p.85)."

From the book of Roy **Cohn,** the assistant of Senator **McCarthy**: "By the middle of 1930's, Communist intrusion into American life was an established fact" (p.3).

However America has survived and won. Moreover she helped the USSR to stand against the fascist Germany.

Watkins again: "Perhaps one of the most reassuring - if occasionally unnerving - aspects of life during the Great

Depression was the fact that millions of Americans, out of work, out of money, sometimes without food and shelter, refused to succumb to despair even in the most harrowing months of the crisis" (p.79).

Then the World War II had come where two psychopaths had destroyed millions of people, ruined many fates, hopes, and all for nothing.

Fascist Germany and its ally Japan gathered each a huge amount of troops. Owing to heroism and self-sacrifice of Soviet and American soldiers and officers the Victory was reached. And glory to the great commanders who led troops in Europe, Far East and Africa - Russian marshal **Zhukov**, American generals **Eisenhower** and **MacArthur**.

Famous Russian poet **Brodsky** devoted his poem to marshal **Zhukov**. Here is one very touching piece from the poem.

ON THE DEATH OF ZHUKOV
Never again in the good noble cause
Zhukov won't put his right hand in combat.
Sleep! Russian history pages
Will keep the names who in infantry lines
Fearlessly entered the foreigner Capital-cities
Seized by the fear to return in their own one (p. 240).

And then the new attack on freedom. The battle in the Hollywood after the World War II to prevent a strike has begun. The President of the Screen Actors Guild of this time: "The Communist plan for Hollywood was remarkably simple. It was merely to take over the motion picture business. Not only for its profit, as the hoodlums had tried - but also for a grand world-wide propaganda base. The Communists were among those who reacted in Hollywood by distorting any facts they got, claiming they were victims of a "blacklist" - when they were actually working members of a conspiracy directed by Soviet Russia against the United States (p.162)." This is from the book of Ronald **Reagan** *Where's the Rest of Me?*

In my opinion Ronald Reagan first of all was the very decent man. The wicked tongues are trying to diminish his value as a Hollywood star. I can only recommend to watch his movie *Kings Row.*

Ronald **Reagan** was the first from highest rank state leaders who discerned the real nature of the communists. After the victory over the strike-makers Ronald **Reagan** in his book *An American Life* wrote: "Now I knew from firsthand experience how Communists used lies, deceit, violence, or other tactic that suited them to advance the cause of Soviet expansionism. I knew from the experience of hand-to-hand combat that America faced no more insidious of evil threat than that of Communism (p.115)."

American red professors, remember this, please. For your entertainment I propose some half-joke.

Famous Russian poet Yevgeniy **Yevtushenko** is reasoning in his book *A Precocious Autobiography* about the real and unreal communists. As the example of the real communist he depicted the father of one of his school friend. It was "a man high up in a trade organization, pompously quoting **Lenin**'s words: 'Under communism we will use gold to build latrines.' The quotation delighted me. But on the day of the currency reform[93], my friend's father was found dead. He

---

93 1947 currency reform in the USSR: old rubles have been exchanged till definite date as 10:1. Many people especially those who illegally made big money had a crash.

had shot himself and lay beside a gutted mattress stuffed with devalued rubles."

To-day the pendulum is turning to the socialism again. However what is so ridiculous that this new economical and political wave is typical for America, not for Russia.

It is not necessary to compile big volumes to understand that fair distribution of world resources is impossible because they are not enough for everybody, who wants to live not worse than his neighbor, to have a luxury car and a very big house.

Anytime in the world history there were greedy and egocentric individuals who wanted and want now to obtain unlimited power over their subjects. Actually the socialism, the communism are the modifications of the slavery.

Ronald **Regan** from his book *An American Life:* "In the early 1980s, Soviet Communism was not just another competing economic system run by people who happened to disagree with us about the merits of capitalism and free enterprise. It was a predatory system of absolute, authoritarian rule that had an insatiable appetite for expansion; it was determined to impose tyranny wherever it went, rob people of fundamental human rights, destroy democratic governments, subvert churches and labor unions, turn the courts and the press into instruments of dictatorship, forbid free elections, imprison and execute critics without charge or trial, and reward the few at the top of the monolith with the spoils of corruption and dictatorial rule. In short, it was against everything Americans have stood for more than two hundred years (p.471)."

Americans had stood for the capitalism which is only one able to make real freedom for everybody. But now the capitalism, not only the very conception, is being shaking from all sides. New "crisis" has been "revealed."

Once upon a time when a soccer game was young every team had five forwards, two halfbacks and three defenders, and the main tactical conception in the defense was 'player-to-player' marking: right defender charged left forward from the opponent team, left defender - right forward, center defender - center forward, right halfback - left insight, left halfback - right insight. One very talented Russian soccer coach decided to make the modification of the scheme and to use it from time to time. The forwards of his team did not attack straight by their vertical 'corridors' in the soccer field but changed unexpectedly their directions of the attack aiming to entangle the defenders and the halfbacks from the opponent team. This tactical modification in attack got the name "well-organized disorder."

I am inclined to give the same name to current "crisis." It is very good opportunity to make a lot of extra money by persons who have already a lot of money, to multiply their reaches due to the financial speculations, receiving so called stabilizing Government funds, diminishing the personal in the offices and the enterprises. As well-known proverb says "Poverty is in want of much, avarice - of everything." As one Chicagoan expressed himself: "Culture of greed is the real problem" (*Chicago Sun-Times*, March 20, 2009, p.21). And the former USSR inhabitants have added the joke: "Everywhere you come to the New Year's party the tables are crammed with the financial crisis". And it is very convenient for a new power to start from "ruins." It would be much more easily to cure the "bad economy."

In this place it is very difficult not to cite the great American again: "But then came the newfangled 'liberals' that claimed government had a greater wisdom than individuals to determine what was best for the individual and it should engineer our economic and business life according to its goals and values; dictate to states, cities, and towns what their rights and responsibilities were; and take an increasing bite out of the earnings of productive workers and redistribute it to those who are not productive (Ronald **Reagan** *An American Life*, p.135).”

One more expression: “When are those fat cats ever satisfied?” I think, there is no more pure socialism, capitalism, imperialism. The international financial whales friendly and confidently are strolling to the new world formation THE CORRUPTIONISM, using the formula: “The bigger amount of richness you divide on the lesser amount of persons the more you get!”

What could we done, the old and young intelligent. I think just to influence the people to try to implement the better understanding real life problems, the solidarity of decent human beings.

“INTELLIGENTS OF THE WORLD UNITE!”

VOCABULARY

* AIDS – the Acquired Immunodeficiency Syndrome.
* Anecdote – very popular in Russia, Ukraine small funny story with witty and unexpected end.
* Bolsheviks - the members of the party which made in Russia the October upheaval (1917), ruled Russia, then Soviet Union till 1990. From about 1930 these members received one more name 'Communists' as the members of the Communist Party of the Soviet Union (CPSU).
* Borzhom - Caucasian mineral water.
* Caucasus, the – area around the range of Caucasian mountains between Black and Caspian seas.
* Chakras – a Sanskrit (one of the 22 official languages of India) word that is translated as 'wheel' or 'disc'. The Chakras are said to be 'force centers' of energy permeating from a point on the physical body.
* Chernobyl disaster – a nuclear reactor incident in the Chernobyl Nuclear Power Plant in the Soviet Union (now Ukraine) on April 26, 1986.
* Communists - the members of the Communist Party of the Soviet Union (CPSU).
* Cosmopolitans - at the end of 1948 Soviet propaganda has begun the official campaign against cosmopolitanism which labeled the people (mostly Jewish) who happened to show the positive attitude to the foreign valuables as the 'persons without kith or kin', 'rootless cosmopolitans'. At the same

time there were widespread dismissals and arrests of Jews in universities and other institutions.

* CPSU - Communist Party of the Soviet Union.

* Crimea - the peninsula of the southern Ukraine, circled by Black sea on the West, South and East.

* Dissertation – a scientific work that has to be defended in public to receive a scientific degree of candidate or doctor of science.

* Dnieper - the biggest river in the Ukraine.

* GDR (in German language - DDR) - after World War II the Germany was divided on two parts: the Federal Republic of Germany, free capitalist country, and the German Democratic Republic with strong influence of the USSR.

* Impostor – the false Dmitriy; a tramp, fugitive deacon by the real name Yuriy (Grigoriy) **Otrep'ev** who pretended to be Tsarevich Dmitriy, the son of the Tsar Ivan the Terrible. Young Dmitriy was brutally killed in 1591 being nine years old by the order of Boris **Godunov**. Impostor ruled Russia as a Tsar in 1605-1606. In his fight for the Russian throne he was supported by Lithuanian and Polish noblemen.

* Inferiority complex - a feeling that one is inferior to others in some way. Such feelings can arise from an imagined or actual inferiority in the afflicted person. It is mostly subconscious, and can drive afflicted individuals for overcompensation, resulting in spectacular achievement, or for a retreat from difficulties, or causes an extreme schizophrenic behavior.

* KGB - the Russian Committee of State Security (abbreviation by the first Russian letters).

* Kiev City - the capital of the Ukraine, was founded early in the 6th century A.C. by brothers Kiy, Shchek and Choriv, and their sister Lybid; the city was named after the eldest

brother Kiy. The first dated mention of the city refers to 862 A.C. when Kiev was ruled by princes Askold and Dir.

* Kiev-Pechersk monastery - in 1051 A.C. the monks Anthony and Theodosius founded a cave monastery over the Dnieper River by name Kiev-Pechersk Lavra.

* Komsomol - the Youth Communist Union.

* Kremlin (Moscow Kremlin) - the historic fortified complex at the heart of the Moscow City, the symbol of the Soviet power, now the Russian highest authorities.

* Meditation – the mental technique by which the person attempts to get beyond the conditioned thinking mind to a deeper state of relaxation.

* Moscow - the capital of the Russia. The first Russian reference to the Moscow City is 1147 A.C.; the founder of the city is Prince Yuriy **Dolgorukiy** (1099-1157) who was buried at Church of Our Savior in Kiev-Pechersk monastery.

* October 1917 upheaval – Bolsheviks have organized revolutionary workers, peasants, soldiers and sailors to take power in Russia by arms.

* Odessa - Ukrainian city on the shore of the Black sea.

* Perestroyka (has begun in 1988) - the policy of restructuring the economic and political system; was promoted by Mikhail Sergeyevich **Gorbachev** (born 1931), General Secretary of the CPSU from 1985, president of the USSR from 1988.

* Plavki - this Russian word has two meanings: 1) smelted metal for one production cycle, 2) swimming trunks.

* Pravda - the main newspaper of the CPSU.

* Red Army - Bolsheviks' military forces during Russian Civil War.

* Red Square - a place beside the Moscow Kremlin, the symbol of the Soviet, now the Russian highest authorities.

* Rest house - the kind of resort facility in the former Soviet Union.
* Ruble - Russian currency.
* Russian Civil War (1917-1923) - the war within the former Russian Empire after October upheaval between the Bolsheviks' Red Army and the anti-Bolshevik's White Army.
* Sanatorium - a resort facility with medical treatment.
* Slavs - the ancestors of the Russian people; the name 'Slavs' is derived from Russian word 'Slava' which means glory.
* Sochi - very fashionable Russian resort in the Caucasus, on the shore of the Black sea.
* Socialistic camp - a number of Eastern European countries which were under the influence of the USSR after the World War II till about 1990. It included Bulgaria, Czechoslovakia, German Democratic Republic, Hungary, Poland, Romania, in some degree - Albania and Yugoslavia.
* Soviet (the adjective) - this word is derived from the Russian word 'Sovet' (Soviet, the noun), the primary form of the state power after Bolsheviks' uprising in 1917: the Soviet of Workers', Peasants' and Red Army men's Deputies. The word 'soviet' is the symbol of the Soviet power, soviet style of life.
* Soviet Union - short name for the Union of the Soviet Socialistic Republics, had the abbreviation 'the USSR'.
* Tsar – the supreme ruler of the Russia,
* Ukraine - the independent state situated geographically between Russia and Poland.
* USSR - the Union of the Soviet Socialistic Republics (Soviet Union).
* Varangians - one of the group of Scandinavian seafarers.
* Vodka - a very strong Russian alcoholic beverage invented by the outstanding Russian scientist **Mendeleyev.**

* Volga River - great Russian river, the largest river in the Europe; Russian people have a great feeling for the river.
* White Army - anti-Bolsheviks Army during Russian Civil War.
* Yalta - Ukrainian resort in Crimea, on the shore of the Black sea.

NAME DIRECTORY

Russian names have a format: last name, first name, patronymic name.

All last names are highlighted.

* **Andersen**, Hans Christian (1805-1875) – great Danish writer of fairy tales

* **Andropov** Yuriy Vladimirovich (1914-1983) - General Secretary of the CPSU in 1982-1983.

* **Babel** Isaak Emmanuilovich (1894-1940) - well-known Soviet writer, was shot after being accused in anti-soviet activity.

* **Bach**, Johann Sebastian (1685-1750) - great German composer.

* **Balanchine**, George (**Balanchivadze** Georgiy Melitonovich) (1904-1983) - born in Saint Petersburg in Russia, Georgian origin – outstanding choreographer who revolutionized ballet.

* **Bebel**, August Ferdinand (1840-1913) - German social democrat, one of the founders of the Social Democratic Party of the Germany.

* **Bedny**, Demyan (1883-1945) - an orthodox, "proletarian" poet (as he was called by officials). Nevertheless on one occasion he was severely criticized for the libretto of an opera *Bogatyri* (heroes in Russian folklore) which displeased Communist party. The libretto satirized the conversion of Russia into Christianity by the prince Vladimir in 988 AC.

* **Bismarck**, prince Otto von (1815-1898) - great statesman who united Germany into a single nation; was named "Iron Chancellor."
* **Bonaparte** Napoleon (1769-1821) – famous French Emperor.
* **Botkin**, Sergey Petrovich (1832-1889) - famous Russian clinician.
* **Brezhnev**, Leonid Ilyich (1906-1982) - General Secretary of the CPSU in 1964-1982.
* **Briand**, Aristide (1862-1932) – French premier eleven times, famous for his efforts toward world peace; in 1926 he won the Nobel peace prize for his work to prevent wars in Europe.
* **Brodsky**, Iosif Aleksandrovich (1940-1996) - famous Russian poet, well-known abroad, won the Nobel Prize in Literature in 1987. In 1963 he was charged for parasitism (one of the technique to break the high-talented people who were not an adherent of soviet ideology), sentenced to five years of internal exile with obligatory engagement in physical work. After protests of soviet and foreign literary figures his sentence was commuted in 1965. Brodsky was expelled from the USSR in 1972 and moved to the United States where he was naturalized in 1977. Most of Brodsky's writings were published in the West.
* **Bryusov**, Valeriy Yakovlevich (1873-1924) - Russian symbolist poet.
* **Bunin**, Ivan Alekseyevich (1870-1953) - great Russian writer, defected from red Russia in 1919; in 1933 won the Nobel Prize in Literature.
* **Casey**, William (1913-1987) – Director of the CIA in 1981-1987 who intensified the agency's anti-communist adtivities.

* **Chapayev**, Vasiliy Ivanovich (1887-1919) – the legendary Bolshevik's Red Army commander, the Hero of the Russian Civil War.

* **Chekhov**, Anton Pavlovich (1868-1903) - great Russian writer and play-writer, well-known in the USA.

* **Cohn**, Roy Marcus (1927-1986) - lawyer, the chief counselor to Senator Joseph **McCarthy**.

* **Corvalan**, Luis Alberto (born 1916) - former General Secretary of the Communist Party of Chile. After military coup in Chile in 1973 he was imprisoned, and in 1976 was exchanged for a notable Soviet political prisoner, dissident **Bukovsky**, Vladimir Konstantinovich (born 1942).

* **Duncan,** Isadora (1878-1927) - famous American dancer, who developed a new kind of dancing; was the wife of the outstanding Russian poet **Esenin**.

* **Ehrenburg**, Ilya Grigoryevich (1891-1967) – famous Soviet writer.

* **Einstein**, Albert (1879-1955) - one of the greatest scientist of all times, the founder of the theory of relativity.

* **Eisenhower**, Dwight David (1890-1969) - 34th President of the United States, Supreme Commander of all Allied forces in Europe in World War II.

* **Esenin**, Sergey Aleksandrovich (1895-1925) - outstanding Russian poet, committed suicide.

* **Feuerbach**, Ludwig Andreas (1804-1872) - outstanding German philosopher.

* **Freud**, Sigmund (1856-1939) – the greatest psychologist of all times and people, founder of psychoanalysis.

* **Funes** de, Louis (1914-1983) – one of the giants of French comedy.

* **Gippius**, Zinaida Nikolayevna (1869-1945) - well-known Russian poetess, defected from red Russia in 1919 (her book see in the *Literature.)*

* **Gogol**, Nikolay Vasilyevich (1809-1852) - the great and very original writer who was born in the Ukraine; wrote his literature works in Russian language.

* **Hegel**, Georg Wilhelm Friedrich (1770-1831) - the distinguished German philosopher.

* **Hitler**, Adolf (real name **Schicklgruber**) (1889-1945) – founder of the German National Socialist Party (Nazi Party); dictator, conqueror, wild anti-Semite; by his order many Jews were destroyed in German concentration camps.

* *Ivan* – the most popular Russian first name.

* *Ivan the Terrible* - Russian Tsar Ivan the Fourth "Terrible", ruled 1533-1584. In 1582 he killed his oldest son Ivan, the heir of the Russian throne.

* **Ivanov** – the most popular Russian last name.

* **Ivinskaya**, Olga Vsevolodovna (born 1912) - mistress and collaborator of **Pasternak**, partly model for Lara, the heroine of *Doctor Zhivago*; in 1949 she served four years in a forced labor camp on the ground of a political accusation. In 1960, after two months of **Pasternak**'s death, she was sentenced to eight years of forced labor camp; her daughter Irina was sentenced for three years of forced labor camp. It was communists' posthumous retaliation upon the great writer.

* **Keldysh**, Mstislav Vsevolodovich (1911-1978) - mathematician and mechanic, president of the Soviet Academy of Sciences in 1961-1975.

* **Kaganovich**, Lazar Moiseevich (1893-1991) - former Secretary of the Central Committee of the CPSU.

* **Karamzin**, Nikolay Mikhailovich (1766-1826) - the outstanding Russian historian.

* **Khrushchev**, Nikita Sergeyevich (1894-1971) - the General Secretary of the CPSU in 1953-1964.

* **Konstantinov** – popular Russian last name.

* **Krylov**, Ivan Andreyevich (1769-1844) - the outstanding Russian fabulist.

* **Le Bon**. Gustav (1841-1931) – the great French historian and psychologist.

* **Lenin**, Vladimir Ilyich (real name '**Ulyanov**') (1870-1924) - the leader of the October 1917 upheaval in the Russia, founder of the USSR and the Communist party.

* **Lermontov**, Mikhail Yurievich (1814-1841) – great Russian poet, perished in a duel.

* **Lobanovskiy**, Valeriy Vasil'evich (1939-2002) - outstanding Ukrainian soccer player and coach; born in Kiev City, graduated high school being awarded by a silver medal; then graduated technical institute and physical culture institute.

* **MacArthur**, Douglas (1880-1964) - a General of the Army, one of the America's greatest military heroes in World War II, Commander of all United States forces in the Pacific campaign against Japan.

* **Malenkov**, Georgiy Maksimilianovich (1902-1988) - top Communist Party leader, in 1953-1955, First Secretary of the CPSU.

* **Mandelstam**, Nadezhda Yakovlevna (1899-1980) - wife of the prominent Russian poet **Mandelshtam**. Her books about her husband: *Hope Against Hope* (1970), *Hope Abandoned* (1974).

* **Mandelstam**, Osip Emilyevich (1891-1938) - prominent Russian poet; perished in Soviet concentration camp after second arrest in 1938.

* **Marais**, Jean (1913-1998) – the outstanding French movie actor.

* **Marx**, Karl (1818-1883) - German economist and philosopher, the founder of the theory of the 'scientific communism'.

* **Mayakovskiy**, Vladimir Vladimirovich (1893-1930) - famous Soviet poet, committed suicide.

* **McCarthy**, Josef Raymond (1908-1957) - Republican Senator from Wisconsin in 1947-1957, main investigator of subversive un-American activities.

* **Mendeleyev**, Dmitriy Ivanovich (1834-1907) –the outstanding Russian chemist and inventor, creator of the periodic table of elements; also formulated new standards for the production of vodka and revealed that the spiritualists during their sessions involuntary simultaneously touch the bottom of the table by their fingers that cause the table rotation.

* **Mikhalkov**, Sergey Vladimirovich (1913-2009) - famous soviet poet, coauthor of the lyrics to the soviet anthem.

* **Molotov**, Vyacheslav Mikhaylovich (1890-1986) a leading figure in the Soviet government from 1920, many years the Foreign minister of the USSR.

* **Moritz**, Yunna Petrovna (born 1937) - Russian artist of many talents, primarily known as a poet.

* **Nagibin**, Yuriy Markovich (1920-1998) – the famous Russian writer.

* **Nekrasov**, Nikolay Alekseyevich (1821-1878) - the great Russian poet.

* **Nestor** - ancient chronicler, the monk of Kiev-Pechersk monastery (lived in XI A.C. century), named as "the father of Russian history."

* **Nietzsche**, Friedrich Wilhelm (1844-1900) - great German philosopher.

* **Pasternak**, Boris Leonidovich (1890-1960) - distinguished Russian poet, writer, created *Doctor Zhivago*, the most striking "anti-Soviet" literary work. The Soviet authorities could not forgive him this action and not being able to deal with, imprisoned after his death two very dear for him women (see above in the name 'Ivinskaya' and the book written by her).

* *Peter I, the Great* (1672-1725) – Russian Emperor in 1682-1725. In 1718 his eldest son and heir Alexey had been tortured and killed on his order.

* **Perrot**, Jules (1810-1892) - French ballet master, in 1849 arrived in Saint Petersburg having been accepted in the position of Premier Maitre de Ballet of the Saint Petersburg Imperial Theatres.

* **Petipa,** Marius (1818-1910) - French ballet dancer, teacher, choreographer, ballet master, was officially named Premier Maitre de Ballet of the Saint Petersburg Imperial Theatres in 1871.

* **Pugacheva**, Alla Borisovna (born in 1949) - very popular Russian female pop-singer.

* **Pushkin**, Alexander Sergeyevich (1799-1837) - great Russian poet, universally recognized as a founder of the contemporary Russian language.

* **Radzinskiy**, Edward Stanislavovich (born 1944) contemporary Russian writer and play writer.

* **Saint-Leon**, Arthur (1821-1870) - the renowned French ballet master, received in 1860 the position of Premier Maitre de Ballet of the Saint Petersburg Imperial Theatres.

* **Saroyan**, William (1908-1981) - famous American writer of Armenian origin.

* **Shepilov**, Dmitriy Trofimovich (1905-1995) - Soviet politician and Foreign minister, joined the abortive plot to oust **Khrushchev** from power in 1957 together with **Malenkov**, **Molotov** and **Kaganovich**.

* **Shevchenko**, Taras Grigoryevich (1814-1861) - great Ukrainian national poet, painter, graphic artist. He was born as a serf. With the help of Russian writers and artists he was bought out of the serfdom. For the Ukrainian nationalism ideas spent 10 years in the exile with the military duty and the prohibition to write and to paint. The Kiev-City University bears his name.

* **Solzhenitsyn**, Alexander Isayevich (1918-2008) - the outstanding Russian writer; was in the Soviet army in the field during World War II. At the end of the war he was imprisoned for "anti-Soviet propaganda", and was put in the concentration camp. He was the first who informed West about the horrors of the Soviet concentration camps.

* **Stalin**, Iosif Vissarionovich (real name **Djugashvili**) (1879-1953) - professional revolutionary, was born in the Caucasian Georgia; dictator of the USSR.

* **Stanislavskiy**, Konstantin Sergeyevich (1863-1938) - outstanding Russian theatrical director.

* **Stekel**, Wilhelm (1868-1940) - one of the most talented and distinguished disciples of **Freud**.

* **Tjutchev**, Fyodor Ivanovich (1803-1873) - famous Russian poet.

* **Tolstoy**, Alexey Konstantinovich, count (1817-1875) - famous Russian poet, novelist, dramatist.

* **Ukrainka**, Lesya (**Kosach**, Larisa Petrivna) (1871-1913) – great Ukrainian national poetess; from the childhood she suffered for hard disease (spinal tuberculosis).

* **Virskiy**, Pavel Pavlovich (1905-1975) - innovative dancer, ballet master, choreographer, founder of the Pavel **Virsky** Ukrainian National Folk Dance Ensemble.

* **Wells**, Herbert George (1866-1946) - famous English writer.

* **Wiener**, Norbert (1894-1964) - great American mathematician, the Father of Cybernetics.

* **Wrangel** - baron Pyotr Nikolayevich **Wrangel** (1878-1928), an officer of the Imperial Russian army, later commanding general of anti-Bolshevics White Army that opposed the Bolsheviks after the October upheaval.

* **Yevtushenko**, Yevgeniy Aleksandrovich (born in 1933) - famous Russian poet, now teaches Russian literature in the USA.

* **Zhukov**, Georgiy Konstantinovich (1896-1974) - Marshal of the Soviet Union, outstanding commander of the Soviet military forces during the World War II. Many people, especially in the XX century, considered him the one who saved Motherland from the fascists.

LITERATURE

* **Andrews**, Robert. *The New Penguin Dictionary of Modern Quotations*. New York, London: Penguin Books, 2000.
* **Brodskiy**, Iosif. *The Volte-face of the Empire*. Moscow: Nezavisimaya Gazeta, 2001 (in Russian language).
* **Bunin**, Ivan. *Cursed Days: A Diary of Revolution*. Chicago: Ivan R. Dee, 1998.
* **Cohn**, Roy. *McCarthy*. New York: New American Library, 1968.
* **Ehrenburg**, Ilya. *Extraordinary Adventures*. St. Petersburg: Crystal, 2001 (in Russian language).
* **Eyck**, Erich. *Bismarck and the German Empire*. London: Allen &Unwin, 1958.
* **Gippius**, Zinaida Nikolayevna. *Alive faces*. Moscow: Olma-Press, 2002 (in Russian language).
* **Ivinskaya,** Olga. *A Captive of Time*. Garden City, New York: Doubleday, 1978.
* **Karamzin** Nikolay Mikhailovich. *The History of the State of Russia*. Moscow: Eksmo, 2007 (in Russian language).
* **Kerner**, Ian. *She Comes First: The Thinking Man's Guide To Pleasuring a Woman*. New York: Collins Living, 2004.
* **Kerner**, Ian. *He comes Next: The Thinking Woman's Guide To Pleasuring a Man. New York: Collins, 2006.*
* **Latyshev** A.G. *Declassified Lenin*. Moscow: MART, 1996 (in Russian language).

* **Le Bon**, Gustav. *The Psychology of Socialism*. Wells, Vermont: Fraser Publishing Group, 1965 (first French edition in 1896).

* **Lewis**, Ben. *Hammer and Tickle: A History of Communism Told Through Communist Jokes*. London: Weidenfeld & Nicolson, 2008.

* **Mandelstam**, Nadezhda. *Hope Against Hope*. New York: Modern Library, 1999 (first published in 1970).

* **Nagibin**, Yuriy. *The urgent business trip, or Dear Margaret Thatcher*. Selected works, volume 3, Moscow: Agraf, 1996 (in Russian language).

* **Nietzsche**, Friedrich. *Thus Spoke Zarathustra: A Book for All and None*. New York: Modern Library, 1995.

* **Palmer**, Alan. *Alexander I: Tsar of War and Peace*. New York: Harper & Row, 1974.

* **Pasternak**, Boris. *Doctor Zhivago*. New York: Pantheon, 1958.

* **Radzinskiy**, Edward. *I stand by the restaurant: to marry - too late, to croak - too early: A monologue of a woman*. Works, vol.3, Moscow: Vagrius, 1998 (in Russian language).

* **Reagan**, Ronald. *Where's The Rest of Me?* New York: Karz Pubs, 1981.

* **Reagan**, Ronald. *An American Life*. New York: Simon & Shuster, 1990.

* **Saroyan**, William. *The Daring Young Man on the Flying Trapeze and Other Stories*. London: Faber & Faber,1935.

* **Toland**, John. *Adolf Hitler*. New York: Balantine Books, 1976.

* **Tolstoy**, A.K. *The History of the State of Russia from Gostomysl till Timashev*. Works in 4 volumes, volume 1, Moscow: Pravda, 1980 (Novgorod prince Gostomysl,

9 century; Timashev, A.E., the minister for internal affairs, 19 century) (in Russian language).

* **Walker**, Charles R., **Guest**, Robert H. *The Man on the Assembly Line*. Cambridge Massachusetts, 1952.

* **Watkins**, T.H. *The Great Depression: America in the 1930s*. Boston: Little Brown, 1993.

* **Wittels**, Fritz. *Sigmund Freud: His Personality, His Teaching and His School*. New York: Books for Libraries Press, 1971 (first published in 1924).

* **Yevtushenko**, Yevgeniy. *A Precocious Autobiography*. New York: Dutton, 1963.

www.ingramcontent.com/pod-product-compliance
Lightning Source LLC
Chambersburg PA
CBHW051411280526
45785CB00003B/1025